THE DUTY OF PASTORS

By John Owen

G|H
www.gideonhousebooks.com

PREFATORY NOTE.

THE title-page of the following treatise indicates that it was published in the year 1644; but in the second chapter of "The Review of the True Nature of Schism," in this volume, it is stated that the date is a misprint for 1643. The work is dedicated to Sir Edward Scot, in whose family, it would appear, the author had for some time resided, and who had offered him some "ecclesiastical preferment" when it was vacant. Owen here declares himself to be in sentiment a Presbyterian, in opposition to Prelacy and Independency. He afterwards changed his views on church- government; but in the work on schism, to which we have just referred, he declares that, on the subjects under discussion in this treatise, his principles had undergone no essential change: "When I compare what I then wrote with my present judgment, I am scarce able to find the least difference between the one and the other."

Two chapters of the work are occupied with a statement of the prevision made for conducting religious instruction and worship under the patriarchal and Mosaic dispensations. An interesting chapter follows on the spiritual priesthood of all believers, as destructive of the superstitions tenet which invests the office of the ministry with esoteric virtue and sanctity. The several ways under which men may be constrained, under an extraordinary call, to impart religious instruction publicly to others, are next considered.

The treatise closes with an assertion of the right and obligation of private Christians to conduct certain kinds of divine worship, without interfering with the official functions of the Christian ministry.

The tractate to which he alludes, "De Sacerdotio Christi contra Armin. Socin. et Papistas," is described as not yet published, and seems never to have been published. It may have supplied part of the long and valuable exercitations on the priesthood of Christ prefixed to the Exposition of the Epistle to the Hebrews, as, from the slight allusion to it in this treatise, the same topics appear to have been handled in it. He refers, also, in the close of this treatise, to an answer, drawn up for the satisfaction of some private friends, to the arguments of the Remonstrants for liberty of prophesying. Mr Orme supposes this unpublished document to be identical with the "Tractatus de Christi Sacerdotio." We are not aware of any grounds for supposing such an identity. The subjects which these unpublished tracts seem to have discussed are obviously different. — ED.

I Have perused this Discourse touching "The Administration of Things Commanded in Religion," and conceive it written with much clearness of judgment and moderation of spirit; and therefore do approve of it to be published in print.

May 11, 1644.
JOSEPH CARYL.

SIR EDWARD SCOT,

OF SCOT'S HALL IN KENT,
KNIGHT OF THE HONORABLE ORDER OF
THE BATH.

Sir,

Having of late been deprived of the happiness to see you, I make bold to send to visit you; and because that the times are troublesome, I have made choice of this messenger, who, having obtained a license to pass, fears no searching. He brings no news, at least to you, but that which was from the beginning, and must continue unto the end, which you have heard, and which (for some part thereof) you have practiced out of the word of God. He hath no secret messages prejudicial to the state of church or commonwealth; neither, I hope, will he entertain any such comments by the way, considering from whom he comes and to whom he goes; of whom the one would disclaim him and the other punish him. Ambitious I am not of any entertainment for these few sheets, neither care much what success they find in their travel, setting them out merely in my own defense, to be freed from the continued solicitations of some honest, judicious men, who were acquainted with their contents, being nothing but an hour's country discourse, resolved from the ordinary pulpit method into its own principles.

When I first thought of sending it to you, I made full account to use the benefit of the advantage in recounting of and returning thanks for some of those many undeserved favors which I have received from you; but addressing myself to the performance, I fainted in the very entrance, finding their score so large that I know not where to begin, neither should I know how to end. Only one I cannot suffer to lie hid in the crowd, though other engagements hindered me from embracing it — namely, your free proffer of an ecclesiastical preferment, then vacant and in your donation. Yet, truly, all received courtesies have no power to oblige me unto you in comparison of that abundant worth which, by experience, I have found to be dwelling in you. Twice, by God's providence, have I been with you when your county hath been in great danger to be ruined, — once by the horrid insurrection of a rude, godless multitude, and again by the invasion of a potent enemy prevailing in the neighbor county; at both which times, besides the general calamity justly feared, particular threatenings were daily brought unto you: under which sad dispensations, I must crave leave to say (only to put you in mind of yourself, if it should please God again to reduce you to the like straits), that I never saw more resolved constancy, more cheerful, unmoved Christian courage in any man. Such a valiant heart in a weak body, such a directing head where the hand was but feeble, such unwearied endeavors under the pressures of a painful infirmity, so well advised resolves in the midst of imminent danger, did I then behold, as I know not where to parallel. Neither can

I say less, in her kind, of your virtuous lady, whose known goodness to all, and particular indulgences to me, make her, as she is in herself, very precious in my thoughts and remembrance: whom having named, I desire to take the advantage thankfully to mention her worthy son, my noble and very dear friend C. Westrow; whose judgment to discern the differences of these times, and his valor in prosecuting what he is resolved to be just and lawful, place him among the number of those very few to whom it is given to know aright the causes of things, and vigorously to execute holy and laudable designs. But farther of him I choose to say nothing, because if I would, I cannot but say too little. Neither will I longer detain you from the ensuing discourse, which I desire to commend to your favorable acceptance, and with my hearty prayers that the Lord would meet you and yours in all those ways of mercy and grace which are necessary to carry you along through all your engagements, until you arrive at the haven of everlasting glory, where you would be. I rest

Your most obliged servant
In Jesus Christ, our common Master,

JOHN OWEN.

CONTENTS

PREFACE

THE glass of our lives seems to run and keep pace with the extremity of time. The end of those "ends of the world"[1] which began with the gospel is doubtless coming upon us. He that was instructed what should be till time should be no more,[2] said it was ἐσχάτη ὥρα,[3] the last hour, in his time. Much sand cannot be behind, and Christ shakes the glass; many minutes of that hour cannot remain; the next measure we are to expect is but "a moment, the twinkling of an eye, wherein we shall all be changed."[4] Now, as if the horoscope of the decaying age had some secret influence into the wills of men to comply with the decrepit world, they generally delight to run into extremes. Not that I would have the fate of the times to bear the faults of men[5] like him who cried, Οὐκ ἐγὼ αἴτιός εἰμι ἀλλὰ Ζεὺς καὶ μοῖρα, to free himself, entitling God and fate to his sins; but only to show how the all-disposing providence of the Most High works such a compliance of times and persons as may jointly drive at his glorious aims, causing men to set out in such seasons as are fittest for their travel. This epidemical disease of the aged world is the cause why, in that great diversity of contrary opinions wherewith

---

[1] 1 Cor. x. 11, Τὰ τέλη τῶν αἰώνων.

[2] Rev. x. 6.

[3] John ii. 18; Matt. xxiv. 33.

[4] 1 Cor. xv. 52; Zanch. de fine sec. Mol. acc. Proph.

[5] Rom. ix. 19.

men's heads and hearts are now replenished, the truth pretended to be sought with so much earnestness may be often gathered up quite neglected between the parties litigant. "Medio tutissimus" is a sure rule, but that fiery spirits, —

"Pyroeis, Eous, et AEthon,
— Quartusque Phlegon," —

will be mounting. In the matter concerning which I propose my weak essay, some would have all Christians to be *almost ministers;* others, *none but ministers* to be God's *clergy.* Those would give the people the keys, these use them to lock them out of the church; the one ascribing to them primarily all ecclesiastical power for the ruling of the congregation, the other abridging them of the performance of spiritual duties for the building of their own souls: as though there were no habitable earth between the valley (I had almost said the pit) of *democratical confusion* and the precipitous rock of *hierarchical tyranny.* When unskilful archers shoot, the safest place to avoid the arrow is the *white.* Going as near as God shall direct me to the truth of this matter, I hope to avoid the strokes of the combatants on every side; and therefore will not handle it ἐριστικῶς, with opposition to any man or opinion, but δογματικῶς, briefly proposing mine own required judgment: the summary result whereof is, that the sacred calling may retain its ancient dignity, though the people of God be not deprived of their Christian liberty. To clear which proposal some things I shall briefly premise.

CHAPTER 1

Of the administration of holy things among the patriarchs before the law.

CONCERNING the ancient patriarchs: From these, some, who would have Judaism to be but an intercision of Christianity,[6] derive the pedigree of Christians, affirming the difference between us and them to be solely in the name, and not the thing itself. Of this, thus much at least is true, that "the law of commandments contained in ordinances"[7] did much more diversify the administration of the covenant before and after Christ than those plain moralities wherewith in their days it was clothed. Where the assertion is deficient, antiquity hath given its authors sanctuary from farther pursuit. Their practice, then, were it clear, can be no precedent for Christians. All light brought to the gospel, in comparison of those full and glorious beams that shine in itself, is but a candle set up in the sun; yet for their sakes who found out the former unity, I will (not following the conceit of any, nor the comments of many) give you such a bare narration, as the Scripture will supply me withal, of their administration of the holy things and practice of their religion (as it seems Christianity, though not so called). And doubt you not

---

[6] *Euseb. Eccles. Hist. lib. i. Cap. 4; Ambr. de Sacra. lib. iv.*
[7] Eph. ii. 15.

of divine approbation and institution; for all prelacy, at least until Nimrod hunted for preferment, was "de jure divino."

I find, then, that before the giving of the law, the chief men among the servants of the true God did, every one in their own families, with their neighbors adjoining of the same persuasion, perform those things which they knew to be required, by the law of nature, tradition, or special revelation (the unwritten word of those times), in the service of God; instructing their children and servants in the knowledge of their creed concerning the nature and goodness of God, the fall and sin of man, the use of sacrifices, and the promised seed (the sum of their religion); and, moreover, performing τὰ πρὸς τὸν Θεόν, things appertaining unto God. This we have delivered concerning Seth, Enoch, Noah, Abraham, Lot, Isaac, Jacob, Jethro, Job, and others.[8] Now, whether they did this as any way peculiarly designed unto it as an office, or rather in obedient duty to the prime law of nature, in which and to whose performance many of them were instructed and encouraged by divine revelation (as seems most probable), is not necessary to be insisted on. To me, truly, it seems evident that there were no determinate ministers of divine worship before the law; for where find we any such office instituted? where the duties of those officers prescribed? or were they of human

---

[8] Gen. iv. 26, v. 22, vi. 8, 9, etc., viii. 20, ix. 25–27, xviii. 19, xix. 9, xxviii. 1, 2, xxxv. 3–5; Exod. xviii. 12; Job i. 5, xlii. 8–10.

invention?[9] God would never allow that in any regard
the will of the creature should be the measure of his
honor and worship. "But the right and exercise of the
priesthood," say some, "was in the first-born;" but a
proof of this will be for ever wanting. Abel was not
Adam's eldest son, yet, if any thing were peculiar to
such an office, it was by him performed. That both
the brothers carried their sacrifices to their father is
a vain surmise.[10] Who was priest, then, when Adam
died? Neither can any order of descent be handsomely
contrived. Noah had three sons: grant the eldest only a
priest; were the eldest sons of his other sons priests, or
no? If not, how many men fearing God were scattered
over the face of the earth utterly deprived of the means of
right worship! if so, there must be a new rule produced
beyond the prescript of nature, whereby a man may be
enabled by generation to convey that to others which
he hath not in himself. I speak not of Melchizedek and
his extraordinary priesthood; why should any speak
where the Holy Ghost is silent? If we pretend to know
him, we overthrow the whole mystery, and run cross to
the apostle, affirming him to be ἀπάτορα ἀμήτορα,
Without father, mother, or genealogy. For so long
time, then, as the greatest combination of men was in
distinct families (which sometimes were very great),[11]
politics and economics being of the same extent, all
the way of instruction in the service and knowledge
of God was by the way of paternal admonition, — for

[9] *Tho. 22, œ. q. 87, ad 3.*
[10] *Jacob. Armin. de Sacerd. Ch. Orat.*
[11] Gen. xiv. 14.

3

the discharge of which duty Abraham is commended, Genesis 18:19; whereunto the instructors had no particular engagement, but only the general obligation of the law of nature. What rule they had for their performances towards God doth not appear. All positive law, in every kind, is ordained for the good of community. That then being not, no such rule was assigned until God gathered a people, and lifted up the standard of circumcision for his subjects to repair unto. The world in the days of Abraham beginning generally to incline to idolatry and polytheism,[12] the first evident irreconcilable division was made between his people and the malignants, which before lay hid in his decree. Visible signs and prescript rules were necessary for such a gathered church. This before I conceive to have been supplied by special revelation.

The law of nature a long time prevailed for the worship of the one true God. The manner of this worship, the generality had at first (as may be conceived) from the vocal instruction of Adam, full of the knowledge of divine things; this afterward their children had from them by tradition, helped forward by such who received particular revelations in their generation, such as Noah, thence called "A preacher of righteousness." So knowledge of God's will increased,[13] until sin quite prevailed, and "all flesh had corrupted his way." All apostasy for the most part begins in

---

[12] "Eccles. malignantium." — *Aug, con. Faust. lib. xix. cap. 11.*

[13] "Per incrementa temporum crevit divinæ cognitiones incrementum." — *Greg. Hom. xvi. in Ezek. a med.*

the will, which is more bruised by the fall than the understanding. Nature is more corrupted in respect of the desire of good than the knowledge of truth. The knowledge of God would have flourished longer in men's minds had not sin banished the love of God out of their hearts.

The sum is, that before the giving of the law, every one in his own person served God according to that knowledge he had of his will. Public performances were assigned to none, farther than the obligation of the law of nature to their duty in their own families. I have purposely omitted to speak of Melchizedek, as I said before, having spoken all that I can or dare concerning him on another occasion. Only this I will add: they who so confidently affirm him to be Shem, the son of Noah, and to have his priesthood in an ordinary way, by virtue of his primogeniture, might have done well to ask leave of the Holy Ghost for the revealing of that which he purposely concealed to set forth no small mystery, by them quite overthrown. And he who of late makes him look upon Abraham and the four kings, all of his posterity, fighting for the inheritance of Canaan (of which cause of their quarrel the Scripture is silent), robs him at least of one of his titles, a "king of peace," making him neither king nor peaceable, but a bloody grandsire, that either could not or would not part his fighting children, contending for that whose right was in him to bestow on whom he would.

And thus was it with them in the administration of sacred things: There was no divine determination of the priestly office on any order of men. When things appertaining unto God were to be performed in the name of a whole family (as afterward, 1 Samuel 20:6), perhaps the honor of the performance was by consent given to the first-born. Farther; the way of teaching others was by paternal admonition (so Genesis 18:19); motives thereunto, and rules of their proceeding therein, being the law of nature and special revelation. Prescription of positive law, ordained for the good of community, could have no place when all society was domestical. To instruct others (upon occasion) wanting instruction, for their good, is an undeniable dictate of the first principles of nature, obedience to which was all the ordinary warrant they had for preaching to any beyond their own families; observed by Lot, Genesis 19:7, though his sermon contained a little false doctrine, verse 8. Again; as special revelation leaves a great impression on the mind of him to whom it is made, so an effectual obligation for the performance of what it directeth unto:

> "The lion hath roared, who will not fear? the Lord God hath spoken, who can but prophesy?" Amos 3:8.

And this was Noah's warrant for those performances from whence he was called "A preacher of righteousness," 2 Peter 2:5. Thus, although I do not find any determinate order of priesthood by divine institution, yet do I not thence conclude, with Aquin. 12. ae. quest. 3. a 1. (if I noted right at the reading of it), that all the worship of God (I mean for the manner of it) was of human invention, yea, sacrifices themselves; for this will-worship, as I showed before, God always rejected. No doubt but sacrifices and the manner of them were of divine institution, albeit their particular original in regard of precept, though not of practice, be to us unknown. For what in all this concerns us, we may observe that a superinstitution of a new ordinance doth not overthrow any thing that went before in the same kind, universally moral or extraordinary, nor at all change it, unless by express exception; as, by the introduction of the ceremonial law, the offering of sacrifices, which before was common to all, was restrained to the posterity of Levi. Look, then, what performances in the service of God that primitive household of faith was in the general directed unto by the law of nature, the same, regulated by gospel light (not particularly excepted), ought the generality of Christians to perform; which what they were may be collected from what was fore-spoken.

CHAPTER 2

Of the same among the Jews, and of the duty of that people distinct from their church officers.

CONCERNING the Jews after the giving of Moses' law: The people of God were then gathered in one, and a standard was set up for all his to repair unto, and the church of God became like a city upon a hill, conspicuous to all, and a certain rule set down for every one to observe that would approach unto him. As, then, before the law, we sought for the manner of God's worship from the practice of men, so now, since the change of the external administration of the covenant, from the prescription of God.

Then we guessed at what was commanded by what was done; now, at what was done by what was commanded. And this is all the certainty we can have in either kind, though the consequence from the precept to the performance, and on the contrary, in this corrupted state of nature, be not of absolute necessity; only, the difference is, where things are obscured, it is a safer way to prove the practice of men by God's precept, charitably supposing them to have been obedient, than to wrest the divine rule to their observation, knowing how prone men are to deify themselves by mixing their inventions with the worship of God. The administration of God's providence towards his church hath been various, and the communication of himself unto it, at "sundry times," hath been in "divers manners;" especially, it pleased him not to bring it to perfection but by degrees, as the earth bringeth forth fruit; "first the blade, then the ear, after that the full corn in the ear."[14] Thus, the church, before the giving of Moses' law, seems to have had two main defects, which the Lord at that time supplied; — one in discipline or government, in that every family exercised the public worship of God within itself or apart (though some do otherwise conclude from Genesis 4:26), which was first removed by establishing a consistory of elders; the other in the doctrine, wanting the rule of the written word, being directed by tradition, the manifold defects whereof were made up by a special revelation. To neither of these defects was the church since exposed. Whether there was any thing written before the giving of the law is not worth contending about. Austin thought Enoch's prophecy was written by him;[15] and Josephus affirms that there were two pillars erected, one of stone, the other of brick, before the flood, wherein divers things were engraven;[16] and Sixtus Senensis, that the book of the wars of the Lord was a volume ancienter than the books of Moses; — but the contrary opinion is most received: so *Chrysostom Hom. 1. in Mali.*[17] After its giving, none ever doubted of the perfection of the

---

[14] Mark iv. 28.

[15] *Aug. de Civit. Dei, lib. xv. Cap. 23.*

[16] *Joseph. Antiq. lib. i. cap. 3. Sixt. Senens. Bib. lib. ii.*

[17] The only place in the works of Chrysostom in which we can find this opinion, is in *"Ad. Pop. Antioch., Homil. ix."* It is upon Ps. xix. 1, and "in Mali" seems a misprint for "in 'Cœli, etc.,'"— "Cœli enarrant gloriam Dei." — ED.

written word for the end to which it was ordained, until the Jews had broached their Talmud to oppose Christ, and the Papists their traditions to advance Antichrist; doubtless the sole aim of the work, whatever were the intentions of the workmen.

The lights which God maketh are sufficient to rule the seasons for which they are ordained. As, in creating of the world, God" made two great lights, the greater light to rule the day, and the lesser light to rule the night;" so, in the erection of the new world of his church, he set up two great lights, the lesser light of the Old Testament to guide the night, the dark space of time under the law, and the greater light of the New Testament to rule the glorious day of the gospel. And these two lights do sufficiently enlighten every man that cometh into this new world. There is no need of the false fire of tradition where God sets up such glorious lights. This be premised for the proneness of men to deflect from the golden rule and heavenly pole-star in the investigation of the truth, especially in things of this nature concerning which we treat, wherein ordinary endeavors are far greater in searching after what men have done than what they ought to have done; and when the fact is once evidenced from the pen of a rabbi or a father, presently to conclude the right. Amongst many, we may take a late treatise, for instance, entitled, *"Of Religious Assemblies and the Public Service of God,"*[18] whose author would prescribe

---

[18] Herbert Thorndike, a learned divine, and one of Walton's assistants in the preparation of his Polyglott, published a treatise under this title in 1642. It is clear that it is to this treatise

the manner of God's worship among Christians from the custom of the Jews; and their observations he would prove from the rabbis, not at all taking notice that from such observances they were long ago recalled to the "law and to the testimony," and afterward for them sharply rebuked by Truth itself.[19] Doubtless it is a worthy knowledge to be able, and a commendable diligence, to search into those coiners of curiosities; but to embrace the fancies of those wild heads, which have nothing but novelty to commend them, and to seek their imposition on others, is but an abusing of their own leisure and others' industry. The issue of such a temper seems to be the greatest part of that treatise; which because I wait only for some spare hours to demonstrate in a particular tract, I shall for the present omit the handling of divers things there spoken of, though otherwise they might very opportunely here be mentioned, — as the office and duty of prophets, the manner of God's worship in their synagogues, the original and institution of their later teachers, scribes and Pharisees, etc., and briefly only observe those things which are most immediately conducing to my proposed subject.

The worship of God among them was either moral or ceremonial and typical. The performances belonging unto the latter, with all things thereunto conducing, were appropriated, to them whom God had peculiarly set apart for that purpose. By *ceremonial* worship I understand all sacrifices and offerings, the

---

Owen alludes. — Ed.

[19] Isa. viii. 20; Matt. v., vi.

whole service of the tabernacle, and afterward of the temple; all which were typical, and established merely for the present dispensation, not without purpose of their abrogation, when that which was to be more perfect should appear. Now, the several officers, with their distinct employments in and about this service, were so punctually prescribed and limited by Almighty God, that as none of them might ἀλλοτριοεπισκοπεῖν without presumptuous impiety, intrude into the function of others not allotted to them, as Numbers 16:1-10; so none of their brethren might presume to intrude into the least part of their office without manifest sacrilege, Joshua 22:11-20. True it is, that there is mention of divers in the Scripture that offered sacrifices, or vowed so to do, who were strangers from the priest's office, yea, from the tribe of Levi: as Jephthah, Judges 9.; Manoah, chapter 13; David, 2 Samuel 6., and again, 2 Samuel 24.; Solomon, 1 Kings 3., and again, chapter 9. But following our former rule of interpreting the practice by the precept, we may find, and that truly, that all the expressions of their offerings signify no more but they brought those things to be offered, and caused the priests to do what in their own persons they ought not to perform. Now, hence, by the way, we may observe that the people of God under the New Testament, contradistinct from their teachers, have a greater interest in the performance of spiritual duties belonging to the worship of God, and more in that regard is granted unto them and required of them than was of the ancient people of the Jews, considered as distinguished from their priests, because their duty is prescribed unto them under the notion of these things which then were appropriate only to the priests, as of offering incense, sacrifice, oblations, and the like; which, in their original institution, were never permitted to the people of the Jews, but yet tralatitiously and by analogy are enjoined to all Christians But of these afterward.

The main question is about the duty of the people of God in performances for their own edification, and the extent of their lawful undertakings for others' instruction. For the first, which is of nearest concernment unto themselves, the sum of their duty in this kind may be reduced to these two heads: — *First*, To hear the word and law of God read attentively, especially when it was expounded; secondly, To meditate therein themselves, to study it by day and night, and to get their senses exercised in that rule of their duty: concerning each of which we have both the precept and the practice, God's command and their performance. The one in that injunction given unto the priest, Deuteronomy 31:11-13

> "When all Israel is come to appear before the LORD thy God, in the place which he shall choose, thou shalt read this law before all Israel in their hearing. Gather the people together, men, and women, and children, and thy stranger that is within thy gates, that they may hear, and that they may learn, and fear the LORD your God, and observe to do all the words of this law; and that their children, which have not known, may hear and learn."

All which we find punctually performed on both

sides, Nehemiah 8:1-8. Ezra the priest, standing on a pulpit of wood, read the law and gave the meaning of it; and the "ears of all the people were attentive to the book of the law." Which course continued until there was an end put to the observances of that law; as Acts 15:21,

> "Moses of old time hath in every city them that preach him, being read in the synagogues every sabbath-day."

On which ground, not receding from their ancient observations, the people assembled to hear our Savior teaching with authority, Luke 21:38; and St Paul divers times took advantage of their ordinary assemblies to preach the gospel unto them. For the other, which concerns their own searching into the law and studying of the word, we have a strict command, Deuteronomy 6:6-9,

> "And these words, which I command thee this day, shall be in thine heart: and thou shalt teach them diligently unto thy children, and shalt talk of them when thou sittest in thine house, and when thou walkest by the way, and when thou liest down, and when thou risest up. And thou shalt bind them for a sign upon thine hand, and they shall be as frontlets between thine eyes. And thou shalt write them upon the posts of thy house, and on thy gates."

Which strict charge is again repeated, chapter 11:18, summarily comprehending all ways whereby they might become exercised in the law. Now, because this charge is in particular given to the king, chapter 17:18-20, the performance of a king in obedience thereunto will give us light enough into the practice of the people. And this we have in that most excellent psalm of David, namely, 119.; which for the most part is spent in petitions for light, direction, and assistance in that study, in expressions of the performance of this duty, and in spiritual glorying of his success in his divine meditations; especially, verse 99, he ascribeth his proficiency in heavenly wisdom and understanding above his teachers, not to any special revelation, not to that prophetical light wherewith he was endued (which, indeed, consisting in a transient irradiation of the mind, being a supernatural impulsion, commensurate to such things as are connatural only unto God, doth of itself give neither wisdom nor understanding), but unto his study in the testimonies of God. The blessings pronounced upon and promises annexed to the performance of this duty concern not the matter in hand; only, from the words wherein the former command is delivered, two things may be observed: —

1. That the paternal teaching and instruction of families in things which appertain to God being a duty of the law of nature, remained in its full vigor, and was not at all impaired by the institution of a new order of teachers for assemblies beyond domestical, then established. Neither, without doubt, ought it to cease amongst Christians, there being no other reason why now it should but that which then was not effectual.

Secondly, That the people of God were not only permitted, but enjoined also, to read the Scriptures, and upon all occasions, in their own houses and elsewhere, to talk of them, or communicate their knowledge in them, unto others. There had been then no council at Trent to forbid the one; nor, perhaps, was there any strict canon to bring the other within the compass of a "conventicle." But now, for the solemn public teaching and instructing of others, it was otherwise ordained; for this was committed to them, in regard of ordinary performance, who were set apart by God; as for others before named, so also for that purpose. The author of the treatise I before mentioned concludeth that the people were not taught at the public assemblies by priests as such, — that is, teaching the people was no part of their office or duty; but, on the contrary, that seems to be a man's duty in the service or worship of God which God requires of him, and that appertains to his office, whose performance is expressly enjoined unto him as such, and for whose neglect he is rebuked or punished. Now, all this we find concerning the priests' public teaching of the people; for the proof of which the recital of a few pertinent places shall suffice. Leviticus 10:11, we have an injunction laid upon Aaron and his sons to "teach the children of Israel all the statutes which the LORD had spoken unto them by the hand of Moses." And of the Levites it is affirmed, Deuteronomy 33:10, "They shall teach Jacob thy statutes, and Israel thy law." Now, though some restrain these places to the discerning of leprosies, and between holy and unholy, with their determination of difficulty emergent out of the law, yet this no way impairs the truth of that I intend to prove by them; for even those things belonged to that kind of public teaching which was necessary under that administration of the covenant. But instead of many, I will name one not liable to exception: Malachi 2:7,

> "The priest's lips should keep knowledge, and they should seek the law at his mouth; for he is the messenger of the LORD of hosts;"

— where both a recital of his own duty, that he should be full of knowledge to instruct; the intimation to the people, that they should seek unto him, or give heed to his teaching; with the reason of them both, "For he is the LORD'S messenger" (one of the highest titles of the ministers of the gospel, performing the same office), — do abundantly confirm that instructing of the people in the moral worship of God was a duty of the priestly office, or of the priests as such, especially considering the effect of this teaching, mentioned verse 6, the "turning of many away from iniquity," the proper end of teaching in assemblies: all which we find exactly performed by an excellent priest, preaching to the people on a pulpit of wood, Nehemiah 8:1-8. Farther; for a neglect of this, the priests are threatened with the rejection from their office, Hosea 4:6. Now, it doth not seem justice that a man should be put out of his office for a neglect of that whose performance doth not belong unto it. The fault of every neglect ariseth from the description of a duty. Until something, then, of more force than any thing as yet I have seen be objected to the contrary, we may take it for granted that the teaching of the people under the law in public assemblies was performed ordinarily by the priests, as belonging to their duty and office. Men endued with gifts supernatural, extraordinarily called, and immediately sent by God himself for the instruction of his people, the reformation of his church, and foretelling things to come, — such as were the prophets, who, whenever they met with opposition, stayed themselves upon their extraordinary calling, — come not within the compass of my disquisition. The institution, also, of the schools of the prophets, the employment of the sons of the prophets, the original of the scribes, and those other possessors of Moses' chair in our Savior's time, wherein he conversed here below, being necessarily to be handled in my observations on the fore-named treatise, I shall omit until more leisure and an enjoyment of the small remainder of my poor library shall better enable me. For the present, because treating "in causa facili," although writing without books, I hope I am not beside the truth. The book of truth, praised be God, is easy to be obtained; and God is not tied to means in discovering the truth of that book.

Come we, then, to the consideration of what duty in the service of God, beyond those belonging unto several families, were permitted to any of the people not peculiarly set apart for such a purpose. The ceremonial part of God's worship, as we saw before, was so appropriated to the priests that God usually revenged the transgression of that ordinance very severely. The examples of Uzzah and Uzziah[20] are dreadful testimonies of his wrath in that kind. It was an unalterable law by virtue whereof the priests excommunicated[21] that

---

[20] 2 Sam. vi. 6, 7; 2 Chron. xxvi. 18, 19.
[21] "Cast him out," John ix. 34.

presumptuous king. For that which we chiefly intend, the public teaching of others, as to some it was enjoined as an act of their duty, so it might at first seem that it was permitted to all who, having ability thereunto, were called by charity or necessity. So the princes of Jehoshaphat taught the people out of the law of God, as well as the priests and Levites, 2 Chronicles 17:7-9. So also Nehemiah and others of the chiefs of the people are reckoned among them who taught the people, Nehemiah 8:9. And afterward, when St Paul at any time entered into their synagogues, they never questioned any thing but his abilities; if he had "any word of exhortation for the people," he might "say on."[22] And the scribes, questioning the authority of our Savior for his teaching, were moved to it, not because he taught, but because he taught so and such things, — with authority and against their traditions; otherwise, they rather troubled themselves to think how he should become able to teach, Mark 6:2,3, than him because he did. There are, indeed, many sharp reproofs in the Old Testament of those who undertook to be God's messengers without his warrant; as Jeremiah 22:21,22,

> "I have not sent these prophets, yet they ran; I have not spoken to them, yet they prophesied. But if they had stood in my counsel," etc;

— to which, and the like places, it may satisfactorily be answered, that howsoever, by the way of analogy, they may be drawn into rule for these times of the gospel, yet they were spoken only in reference to them

---

[22] Acts xiii. 15.

who falsely pretended to extraordinary revelations and a power of foretelling things to come, whom the Lord forewarned his people of, and appointed punishments for them, Deuteronomy 13:1-6; with which sort of pretenders that nation was ever replenished, for which the very heathen often derided them. He who makes it his employment to counterfeit God's dispensations had then no more glorious work to imitate than that of prophecy; wherein he was not idle. Yet, notwithstanding all this, I do not conceive the former discourse to be punctually true in the latitude thereof, as though it were permitted to all men, or any men, besides the priests and prophets, to teach publicly at all times, and in all estates of that church. Only, I conceive that the usual answers given to the fore-cited places, when objected, are not sufficient. Take an instance in one, 2 Chronicles 17:7-9, of the princes of Jehoshaphat teaching with the priests. The author of the book before intimated conceives that neither priests nor princes taught at all in that way we now treat of, but only that the priests rode circuit to administer judgment, and had the princes with them to do execution. But this interpretation he borroweth only to confirm his πρῶτον ψεῦδος, that priests did not teach as such. The very circumstance of the place enforces a contrary sense. And in chapter 19:5-7, there is express mention of appointing judges for the determination of civil causes in every city; which evidently was a distinct work, distinguished from that mentioned in this place. And, upon the like ground, I conceive it to be no intimation of a movable sanhedrim; which, although of such a mixed constitution, yet was not itinerant, and is mentioned in that other place. Neither is that other ordinary gloss more probable, "They were sent to teach, that is, to countenance the teaching of the law," — a duty which seldom implores the assistance of human countenance; and if for the present it did, the king's authority commanding it was of more value than the presence of the princes. Besides, there is nothing in the text, nor the circumstances thereof, which should hold out this sense unto us; neither do we find any other rule, precept, or practice, whose analogy might lead us to such an interpretation. That which to me seems to come nearest the truth is, that they taught also, not in a ministerial way, like the priests and Levites, but imperially and judicially, declaring the sense of the law, the offenses against it, and the punishments due to such offenses, especially inasmuch as they had reference to the peace of the commonwealth; which differs not much from that which I rest upon, — to wit, that in a collapsed and corrupted state of the church, when the ordinary teachers are either utterly ignorant and cannot, or negligent and will not, perform their duty, gifts in any one to be a teacher, and consent in others by him to be taught, are a sufficient warrant for the performance of it; and than this the places cited out of the Old Testament prove no more. For the proceedings of St Paul in the synagogues, their great want of teaching (being a people before forsaken of the Spirit, and then withering) might be a warrant for them to desire it, and his apostolical mission for him to do it. It doth not, then, at all from hence appear that there was then any liberty of teaching in public assemblies granted unto or assumed by any, in such an estate of the church as wherein it ought to be. When, indeed, it is ruinously declining, every one of God's servants hath a sufficient warrant to help or prevent the fall; this latter being but a common duty of zeal and charity, the former an authoritative act of the keys, the minister whereof is only an instrumental agent, that from whence it hath its efficacy residing in another, in whose stead, and under whose person it is done, 2 Corinthians 5:19, 20. Now, whoever doth any thing in another's stead, not by express patent from him, is a plain impostor; and a grant of this nature made unto all in general doth not appear. I am bold to speak of these things under the notion of the "keys," though in the time of the law; for I cannot assent to those schoolmen[23] who will not allow that the keys in any sense were granted to the legal priests. Their power of teaching, discerning, judging, receiving in and casting out, import the thing, though the name (no more than that of "regnum coelorum," as Jerome and Augustine observe) be not to be found in the Old Testament; and, doubtless, God ratified the execution of his own ordinances in heaven then as well as now. What the immediate effect of their services was, how far by their own force they reached, and what they typified, how in signification only, and not immediately, they extended to an admission into and exclusion from the heavenly tabernacle, and wherein lies the secret power of gospel

---

[23] Aquin., Durand.

commissions beyond theirs to attain the ultimate end, I have declared elsewhere.[24]

Thus much of what the ancient people of God, distinguished from their priests, might not do; now briefly of what they might, or rather of what they ought, and what their obedience and profession declared that they thought themselves obliged unto. Private exhortations, rebukings, and such dictates of the law of nature, being presupposed, we find them farther "speaking often one to another" of those things which concerned the fear and worship of the Lord, Malachi 3:16; by their "lips feeding many with wisdom," Proverbs 10:21; discoursing of God's laws upon all occasions, Deuteronomy 6:6,7; by multitudes encouraging each other to the service of God, Zechariah 8:20,21,

Isaiah 2:2,3; jointly praising God with cheerful hearts, Psalm 42:4; giving and receiving mutual consolation, Psalm 55:14; and all this, with much more of the same nature, at their meetings, either occasional or for that purpose indicted; — always provided that they abstained from fingering the ark, or meddling with those things which were appropriated to the office of the priests, and concerning them hitherto.

---

[24] *Tractatu de Sacerdotio Christi, contra Armin. Socin. et Papistas,* nondum edito.

CHAPTER 3

Containing a digression concerning the name of "priests," the right of Christians thereunto by their interest in the priesthood of Christ, with the presumption of any particularly appropriating it to themselves.

AND now the transaction of these things in the Christian church presents itself to our consideration; in handling whereof I shall not at all discourse concerning the several church-officers instituted by Christ and his apostles for the edification of his body, nor concerning the difference between them who were partakers at first of an extraordinary vocation and those who since have been called to the same work in an ordinary manner, divinely appointed for the direction of the church. Neither yet doth that diversity of the administration of government in the churches, then when they were under the plenitude of apostolical power, and now when they follow rules prescribed for their reiglement, come in my way.

Farther; who are the subject of the keys, in whom all that secondary ecclesiastical power which is committed to men doth reside, after the determinations of so many learned men by clear Scripture light, shall not by me be called in question. All these, though conducing to the business in hand, would require a large discussion; and such a scholastical handling as would make it an inconsutilous[25] piece of this popular discourse; my intent being only to show, — *seeing there are, as all acknowledge, some under the New Testament, as well as the Old, peculiarly set apart by God's own appointment for the administration of Christ's ordinances, especially teaching of others by preaching of the gospel, in the way of office and duty, — what remaineth for the rest of God's people to do, for their own and others' edification.*

1. But here, before I enter directly upon the matter, I must remove one stone of offense, concerning the common appellation of those who are set apart for the preaching of the gospel. That which is most frequently used for them in the New Testament is διάκονοι, so 1 Corinthians 3:5; 2 Corinthians 3:6, 6:4, 11:15,23; 1 Timothy 4:6, and in divers other places; to which add ὑπηρέται, 1 Corinthians 4:1, a word though of another original, yet of the same signification with the former, and both rightly translated "ministers." The names of "ambassadors," "stewards," and the like, wherewith they are often honored, are figurative, and given unto them by allusion only. That the former belonged unto them, and were proper for them, none ever denied but some Rabshakehs of antichrist. Another name there is, which some have assumed unto themselves as an honor, and others have imposed the same upon them for a reproach, namely, that of "priest;" which, to the takers, seemed to import a more mysterious employment, a greater advancement above the rest of their brethren, a nearer approach unto God, in the performances of

---

[25] Improperly sewn together, not suited to the rest of the discourse. — Ed.

their office, than that of "ministers;" wherefore they embraced it either voluntarily, alluding to the service of God and the administration thereof amongst his ancient people the Jews, or thought that they ought necessarily to undergo it, as belonging properly to them who are to celebrate those mysteries and offer those sacrifices which they imagined were to them prescribed. The imposers, on the contrary, pretend divers reasons why now that name can signify none but men rejected from God's work, and given up to superstitious vanities; attending, in their minds, the old priests of Baal, and the now shavelings of Antichrist. It was a new etymology of this name which that learned man cleaved unto, who, unhappily, was engaged into the defense of such errors as he could not but see and did often confess,[26] — to which, also, he had an entrance made by an archbishop,[27] — to wit, that it was but an abbreviation of "presbyters;" knowing full well, not only that the signification of these words is diverse amongst them to whom belong "jus et norma loquendi," but also that they are widely different in holy writ: yea, farther, that those who first dignified themselves with this title never called themselves presbyters by way of distinction from the people, but only to have a note of distance among themselves, there being more than one sort of them that were sacrificers, and which, "eo nomine," accounted themselves priests. Setting aside, then, all such evasions and distinctions as the people of God are not bound to take notice of,

---

[26] *Hooker's Eccles. Polit. lib. v.*
[27] Whitgift, Ans. to the Admon.

and taking the word in its ordinary acceptation, I shall briefly declare what I conceive of the use thereof, in respect of them who are ministers of the gospel; which I shall labor to clear by these following observations: —

(1.) All faithful ministers of the gospel, inasmuch as they are ingrafted into Christ and are true believers, may, as all other true Christians, be called priests; but this inasmuch as they are members of Christ, not ministers of the gospel. It respecteth their persons, not their function, or not them as such. Now, I conceive it may give some light to this discourse if we consider the grounds and reasons of this metaphorical appellation, in divers places of the gospel ascribed to the worshipers of Christ,[28] and how the analogy which the present dispensation holds with what was established under the administration of the Old Testament may take place; for there we find the Lord thus bespeaking his people, "Ye shall be unto me a kingdom of priests, and an holy nation," Exodus 19:6: so that it should seem that there was then a twofold priesthood; — a ritual priesthood, conferred upon the tribe of Levi; and a royal priesthood, belonging to the whole people. The first is quite abrogated and swallowed up in the priesthood of Christ; the other is put over unto us under the gospel, being ascribed to them and us, and every one in covenant with God, not directly and properly, as denoting the function peculiarly so called, but comparatively, with reference had to them that are without: for as those who were properly called priests

---

[28] Rev. i. 6, v. 10, xx. 6; 1 Pet. ii. 5, 9, etc.

had a nearer access unto God than the rest of the people, especially in his solemn worship, so all the people that are in covenant with God have such an approximation Unto him by virtue thereof, in comparison of them that are without, that in respect thereof they are said to be priests. Now, the outward covenant, made with them who were the children of Abraham after the flesh, was representative of the covenant of grace made with the children of promise, and that whole people typified the hidden elect people of God; so that of both there is the same reason. Thus, as "the priests the sons of Levi" are said to "come near unto God," Deuteronomy 21:5, and God tells them that "him whom he hath chosen, he will cause to come near unto him," Numbers 16:5, — chosen by a particular calling "ad munus," to the office of the ritual priesthood; so in regard of that other kind, comparatively so called, it is said of the whole people,

> "What nation is there so great, who hath God so nigh unto them, as the LORD our God is in all things that we call upon him for?" Deuteronomy 4:7.

Their approaching nigh unto God made them all a nation of priests, in comparison of those "dogs" and unclean Gentiles that were out of the covenant. Now, this prerogative is often appropriated to the faithful in the New Testament: for "through Christ we have access by one Spirit unto the Father," Ephesians 2:18; and chapter 3:12, "We have boldness and access with confidence;" so James 4:8, "Draw nigh to God, and he will draw nigh to you;" — which access and approximation unto God seemed, as before was spoken, to be uttered in allusion to the priests of the old law, who had this privilege above others in the public worship, in which respect only things then were typical; since, because we enjoy that prerogative in the truth of the thing itself, which they had only in type, we also are called priests. And as they were said to "draw nigh" in reference to the rest of the people, so we in respect of them who are "strangers from the covenants," that now are said to be "afar off;" Ephesians 2:17, and hereafter shall be "without;" for "without are dogs," etc, Revelation 22:15. Thus, this metaphorical appellation of priests is, in the first place an intimation of that transcendent privilege of grace and favor which Jesus Christ hath purchased for every one that is sanctified with the blood of the covenant.

(2.) We have an interest in this appellation of priests by *virtue of our union with Christ*. Being one with our high priest, we also are priests. There is a twofold union between Christ and us; — the one, by his taking upon him our nature; the other, by bestowing on us his Spirit: for as in his incarnation he took upon him our flesh and blood by the work of the Spirit, so in our regeneration he bestoweth on us his flesh and blood by the operation of the same Spirit. Yea, so strict is this latter union which we have with Christ, that as the former is truly said to be a union of two natures into one person, so this of many persons into one nature; for by it we are "made partakers of the divine nature," 2 Peter 1:4, becoming "members of his body, of his flesh, and of his bones," Ephesians 5:30. We are so parts of him, of his mystical body, that we and he become thereby, as it were, one Christ: "For as the body is one, and hath many members, and all the members of that one body, being many, are one body: so also is Christ, 1 Corinthians 12:12. And the ground of this is, because the same Spirit is in him and us. In him, indeed, dwelleth the *fullness* of it, when it is bestowed upon us only by *measure*; but yet it is still the *same* Spirit, and so makes us, according to his own prayer, one with him, as the soul of man, being one, makes the whole body with it to be but one man. Two men cannot be one, because they have two souls; no more could we be one with Christ were it not the same Spirit in him and us. Now, let a man be never so big or tall, so that his feet rest upon the earth and his head reach to heaven, yet, having but one soul, he is still but one man. Now, though Christ for the present, in respect of our nature assumed, be never so far remote and distant from us in heaven, yet, by the effectual energy and inhabitation of the same Spirit, he is still the head of that one body whereof we are members, still but one with us. Hence ariseth to us a twofold right to the title of priests: —

(1.) Because being in him, and members of him, we are accounted to have done, in him and with him, whatsoever he hath done for us: We are "dead with him," Romans 6:8; "buried with him," verse 4; "quickened together with him," Ephesians 2:5; "risen with him," Colossians 3:1; being "raised up," we "sit together with him in heavenly places," Ephesians 2:6. Now, all these in Christ were in some sense sacerdotal; wherefore we, having an interest in their performance, by reason of that heavenly participation derived from them unto us, and being united unto him that in them was so properly, are therefore called priests.

(2.) By virtue of this union there is such an analogy between that which Christ hath done for us as a priest and what he worketh in us by his Holy Spirit, that those acts of ours come to be called by the same name with his, and we for them to be termed priests. Thus, because Christ's death and shedding of his blood, so offering up himself by the eternal Spirit, was a true, proper sacrifice for sin, even our spiritual death unto sin is described to be such, both in the nature of it, to be an offering or sacrifice (for, "I beseech you, brethren," saith St Paul, "by the mercies of God, that ye present your bodies a living sacrifice," etc., Romans 12:1), and for the manner of it; our "old man is crucified with him, that the body of sin might be destroyed," Romans 6:6.

(3.) We are priests as we are Christians, or partakers of a holy unction, whereby we are anointed to the participation of all Christ's glorious offices. We are not called Christians for nothing. If truly we are so, then have we an "unction from the Holy One," whereby we "know all things," 1 John 2:20. And thus also were all God's people under the old covenant, when God gave that caution concerning them, "Touch not my CHRISTIANS,[29] and do my prophets no harm," Psalm 105:15. The unction, then, of the Holy Spirit implies a participation of all those endowments

---

[29] Owen here alludes to the meaning of the name, as derived from Christ — "the anointed." — Ed.

which were typified by the anointing with oil in the Old Testament, and invests us with the privileges, in a spiritual acceptation, of all the sorts of men which then were so anointed, — to wit, of kings, priests, and prophets: so that by being made Christians (every one is not so that bears that name), we are ingrafted into Christ, and do attain to a kind of holy and intimate communion with him in all his glorious offices; and in that regard are called priests.

(4.) The *sacrifices* we are enjoined to offer give ground to this appellation. Now, they are of divers sorts, though all in general eucharistical; — as, first, Of prayers and thanksgivings: Psalm 116:17,

> "I will offer unto thee the sacrifice of thanksgiving, and will call upon the name of the LORD;"

and again,

> "Let my prayer be set forth before thee as incense, and the lifting up of my hands as the evening sacrifice." Psalm 141:2:

so Hebrews 13:15, "Let us offer the sacrifice of praise to God," — that is, the "fruit of our lips." Secondly, Of good works: Hebrews 13:16, "To do good and to communicate forget not; for with such sacrifices God is well pleased." Thirdly, Αὐτοθυσίας, or self slaughter, crucifying the old man, killing sin, and offering up our souls and bodies an acceptable sacrifice unto God, Romans 12:1. Fourthly, The sweet incense of martyrdom: "Yea, and if I be offered upon the sacrifice and service of your faith, etc., Philippians 2:17. Now, these and sundry other services acceptable to God, receiving this appellation in the Scripture, denominate the performers of them priests. Now, here it must be observed, that these aforenamed holy duties are called "sacrifices," not properly, but metaphorically only, — not in regard of the external acts, as were those under the law, but in regard of the internal purity of heart from whence they proceed. And because pure sacrifices, by his own appointment, were heretofore the most acceptable service of Almighty God, therefore now, when he would declare himself to be very much delighted with the spiritual acts of our duty, he calls them "oblations," "incense," "sacrifices," "offerings," etc; to intimate, also, a participation with Him in his offices who properly and directly is the only priest of his church, and by the communication of the virtue of whose sacrifice we are made priests, not having authority in our own names to go unto God for others, but having liberty, through him, and in his name, to go unto GOD for ourselves.

Not to lose myself and reader in this digression, the sum is, — The unspeakable blessings which the priesthood of Christ hath obtained for us are a strong obligation for the duty of praise and thanksgiving; of which that in some measure we may discharge ourselves, he hath furnished us with sacrifices of that kind to be offered unto God. For our own parts, we are poor, and blind, and lame, and naked; neither in the field nor in the fold, in our hearts nor among our actions, can we find any thing worth the presenting unto him: wherefore, he himself provides them for us; especially for that purpose sanctifying and consecrating our souls and bodies with the sprinkling of his blood and the unction of the Holy Spirit. Farther; he hath erected an altar (to sanctify our gifts) in heaven, before the throne of grace, which, being spread over with his blood, is consecrated unto God, that the sacrifices of his servants may for ever appear thereon. Add to this, what he also hath added, the eternal and never-expiring fire of the favor of God, which kindleth and consumes the sacrifices laid on that altar. And to the end that all this may be rightly accomplished, he hath consecrated us with his blood to be kings and priests to God for evermore. So that the close of this discourse will be, that all true believers, by virtue of their interest in Jesus Christ, are in the holy Scripture, by reason of divers allusions called priests; which name, in the sense before related, belonging unto them as such, cannot, on this ground, be ascribed to any part of them distinguished any ways from the rest by virtue of such distinction.

2. The second thing I observe concerning the business in hand is, that the offering up unto God of some metaphorical sacrifices, in a peculiar manner, is appropriate unto men set apart for the work of the ministry; as the slaying of men's lusts, and the offering up of them, being converted by the preaching of the gospel, unto God. So St Paul of his ministry,

Romans 15:16,

"That I should be the minister of Jesus Christ unto the Gentiles, ministering the gospel of God, that the offering up of the Gentiles might be acceptable," etc.

Ministers preaching the gospel to the conversion

of souls are said to kill men's lusts, and offer them up unto God as the fruit of their calling, as Abel brought unto him an acceptable sacrifice of the fruit of his flock; and so also in respect of divers other acts of their duty, which they perform in the name of their congregations. Now, these sacrifices are appropriated to the ministers of the gospel, not in regard of the matter, — for others also may convert souls unto God, and offer up prayers and praises in the name of their companions, — but in respect of the manner: they do it publicly and ordinarily; others, privately or in extraordinary cases. Now, if the ministers, who are thus God's instruments for the conversion of souls, be themselves ingrafted into Christ, all the acts they perform in that great work are but parts of their own duty, of the same nature in that regard with the rest of our spiritual sacrifices; so that they have not by them any farther, peculiar interest in the office of the priesthood more than others. But if these preachers themselves do not belong unto the covenant of grace, as God oftentimes, out of his care for his flock, bestows gifts upon some for the good of others, on whom he will bestow no graces for the benefit of their own souls, men may administer that consolation out of the word unto their flock which themselves never tasted, — preach to others, and be themselves cast-aways. St. Paul tells us that some preach Christ out of envy and contention, not sincerely, but on purpose to add to his affliction; and yet, saith he, "whether in pretense, or in truth, Christ is preached; and I therein do rejoice, yea, and will rejoice, Philippians 1:16-18. Surely, had there been no good effected by such preaching, St Paul would not have rejoiced in it; and yet, doubtless, it was no evidence of sanctification to preach Christ merely out of contention, and on purpose to add to the affliction of his servants. But, I say, if the Lord shall be pleased at any time to make use of such as instruments in his glorious work of converting souls, shall we think that it is looked upon as their sacrifice unto God? No, surely. The soul of the Lord is delighted with the repentance of sinners; but all the sacrifices of these wicked men are an abomination unto him, and therefore they have no interest in it. Neither can they from hence be said to be priests of God, seeing they continue "dogs" and "unclean beasts," etc. So that all the right unto this priestly office seems to be resolved into, and to be the same with, the common interest of all believers in Christ, whereby they have a participation of his office. Whence I affirm, —

3. That the name of priests is nowhere in the Scripture attributed *peculiarly and distinctively to the ministers of the gospel as such.* Let any produce an instance to the contrary, and this controversy is at an end. Yea, that which puts a difference between them and the rest of the people of God's holiness seems to be a more immediate participation of Christ's prophetical office, to teach, instruct, and declare the will of God unto men; and not of his sacerdotal, to offer sacrifices for men unto God. Now, I could never observe that any of those who were so forward of late to style themselves priests were at all greedy of the appellation of prophets. No; this they were content to let go, name

37

and thing. And yet, when Christ ascended on high, he gave some to be prophets, for the edification of his body, Ephesians 4:11; none, as we find, to be priests. Priests, then (like prelates), are a sort of church-officers whom Christ never appointed. Whence I conclude, —

4. That whosoever maintaineth any priests of the New Testament as properly so called, in relation to any altar or sacrifice by them to be offered, doth as much as in him lieth *disannul the covenant of grace*, and is blasphemously injurious to the priesthood of Christ. The priest and the sacrifice under the New Testament are one and the same; and therefore, they who make themselves priests must also make themselves Christs, or get another sacrifice of their own. As there is but "one God," so there is but "one mediator between God and men, the man Christ Jesus," 1 Timothy 2:5. Now, he became the mediator of the New Testament chiefly by his priesthood, because "through the eternal Spirit he offered himself to God," Hebrews 9:14,15. Neither is any now called of God to be a priest, as was Aaron; and without such divine vocation to this office none ought to undertake it, as the apostle argues, Hebrews 5:4. Now, the end of any such vocation and office is quite ceased, being nothing but to "offer gifts and sacrifices" unto God, Hebrews 8:3: for Christ hath offered one sacrifice for sins for ever, and is "set down at the right hand of God," chapter 10:12; yea, "by one offering he hath perfected for ever them that are sanctified," verse 14; and if that did procure remission of sins, there must be "no more offering for sin," verse 18; and the surrogation of another makes the blood of Christ to be no better than

that of bulls and goats. Now, one of these they must do who make themselves priests (in that sense concerning which we now treat), — either get them a new sacrifice of their own, or pretend to offer Christ again.[30] The first seems to have been the fault of those of ours who made a sacrifice of the sacrament, yet pretended not to believe the real presence of Christ in or under the outward elements or species of them; the other of the Romanists, whose priests in their mass blasphemously make themselves mediators between God and his Son, and offering up Christ Jesus for a sacrifice, desire God to accept him, — so charging that sacrifice with imperfection which he offered on the altar of the cross, and making it necessary not only that he should annually, but daily, yea hourly, suffer afresh, so recrucifying unto themselves the Lord of glory. Farther; themselves confessing that, to be a true sacrifice, it is required that that which is offered unto God be destroyed, and cease to be what it was, they do confess by what lies in them to destroy the Son of God; and by their mass have transubstantiated their altars into crosses, their temples into Golgothas, their prelates into Pilates, their priests into hangmen, tormentors of Jesus Christ! Concerning them and ours, we may shut up this discourse with what the apostle intimates to the Hebrews, — namely, that all priests are ceased who were mortal. Now, small cause have we to believe them to be immaterial spirits, among whom we find the works of

---

[30] For offering the host, or their Christ, they pray: "Supra quæ, propitio ac sereno vultu respicere digneris, et accepta habere sicut dignatus es munera pueri tui justi Abel, et sacrificium patriarchæ nostri Abrahæ;" with many more to that purpose.

the flesh to have been so frequent.

And this may give us some light into the iniquity of those times whereinto we were lately fallen; in which lord bishops and priests had almost quite oppressed the bishops of the Lord and ministers of the gospel. How unthankful men were we for the light of the gospel! — men that loved darkness rather than light. "A wonderful and horrible thing was committed in the land; the prophets prophesied falsely, the priests bare rule by their means;" almost the whole "people loved to have it so: and what will we now do in the end thereof?" Jeremiah 5:30,31. Such a hasty apostasy was growing on us as we might justly wonder at, because unparalleled in any church, of any age. But our revolters were profound hasty men, and eager in their master's service. So, what a height of impiety and opposition to Christ the Roman apostasy in a thousand years attained unto! and yet I dare aver that never so many errors and suspicions in a hundred years crept into that church as did into ours of England in sixteen. And yet I cannot herein give the commendation of so much as industry to our innovators (I accuse not the whole church, but particulars in it, and that had seized themselves of its authority), because they had a platform before them, and materials provided to their hand, and therefore it was an easy thing for them to erect a Babel of antichristian confusion, when the workmen in the Roman apostasy were forced to build in the plain of Christianity without any pre-existent materials, but were fain to use brick and slime of their own provision. Besides, they were unacquainted with the main design of Satan, who set them on work, and therefore it is no wonder if those Nimrods ofttimes hunted counter, and disturbed each other in their progress. Yea, the first mover in church apostasy knows that now his time is but short, and therefore it behoves him to make speedy work in seducing, lest he be prevented by the coming of Christ.

Then, having himself a long tract of time granted unto him, he allowed his agents to take leisure also; but what he doth now must be done quickly, or his whole design will be quashed: and this made him inspire the present business with so much life and vigor. Moreover, he was compelled then to sow his tares in the dark, "while men slept," — taking advantage of the ignorance and embroilment of the times. If any man had leisure enough to search, and learning enough to see and find him at it, he commonly filled the world with clamors against him, and scarce any but his avowed champions durst be his advocates. In our time he was grown bold and impudent, working at noonday; yea, he openly accused and condemned all that durst accuse him for sowing any thing but good wheat, that durst say that the tares of his Arminianism and Popery were any thing but true doctrine. Let us give so much way to indignation. We know Satan's trade what it is, — to accuse the brethren: as men are called after their professions, one a lawyer, another a physician, so is he "The accuser of the brethren." Now surely, if ever he set up a shop on earth to practice his trade in, it was our High Commission Court, as of late employed; but ἀπέχεσθε.

CHAPTER 4

Of the duty of God's people in cases extraordinary
concerning his worship.

THIS being thus determined, I return again to the main ζητούμενον, concerning the duty and privilege of the common people of Christianity in sacred things; and, first, in cases extraordinary, in which, perhaps, it may be affirmed that every one (of those, I mean, before named) is so far a minister of the gospel as to teach and declare the faith to others, although he have no outward calling thereunto. And yet, in this case, every one for such an undertaking must have a warrant by an immediate call from God. And when God calls there must be no opposition; the thing itself he sends us upon becomes lawful by his mission: "What God hath cleansed, that call not thou common," Acts 10:15. Never fear the equity of what God sets thee upon. No excuses of disability or any other impediment ought to take place; the Lord can and will supply all such defects. This was Moses' case, Exodus 4:10,11: "O my Lord," saith he," I am not eloquent, neither heretofore, nor since thou hast spoken unto thy servant: but I am slow of speech, and of a slow tongue. And the LORD said unto him, Who hath made man's mouth? have not I the LORD?" So also was it with the prophet Jeremiah. When God told him that he had ordained him a prophet unto the nations, he replies,

"Ah, Lord GOD! behold, I cannot speak: for I am a child. But the LORD," saith he, "said unto me, Say not, I am a child: for thou shalt go to all that I shall send thee, and whatsoever I command thee thou shalt speak," Jeremiah 1:6,7.

Nothing can excuse any from going on His message who can perfect his praise out of the mouths of babes and sucklings. This the prophet Amos rested upon when he was questioned, although he were unfit for that heavenly employment either by education or course of life:

"I was no prophet, neither was I a prophet's son; but I was an herdman, and a gatherer of sycomore fruit: and the LORD took me as I followed the flock, and said unto me, Go, prophesy unto my people Israel," Amos 7:14,15.

So, on the contrary, St Paul, a man of strong parts, great learning, and endowments, of indefatigable industry and large abilities, yet affirms of himself that when God called him to preach his word, he "conferred not with flesh and blood," but went on presently with his work, Galatians 1:15-17.

CHAPTER 5

Of the several ways of extraordinary calling to the teaching of others — The first way.

Now, three ways may a man receive, and be assured that he hath received, this divine mission, or know that he is called of God to the preaching of the word; I mean not that persuasion of divine concurrence which is necessary also for them that are partakers of an ordinary vocation, but that which is required in extraordinary cases to them in whom all outward calling is wanting: —

1. By immediate *revelation*;
2. By *a concurrence of Scripture rules* directory for such occasions;
3. By some *outward acts of Providence*, necessitating him thereunto.

For the FIRST, — not to speak of light prophetical, whether it consists in a habit, or rather in a transient irradiating motion, nor to discourse of the species whereby supernatural things are conveyed to the natural faculty, with the several ways of divine revelation (for St Paul affirmeth it to have been πολυτρόπως as well as πολυμερῶς), with the sundry appellations it received from the manner whereby it came, — I shall only show what assurance such a one as is thus called may have in himself that he is so called, and how he may manifest it unto others. That men receiving any revelation from God had always an assurance that such it was, to me seems most certain: neither could I ever approve the note of Gregory on Ezekiel 1., — namely, "That prophets, being accustomed to prophesying, did oftentimes speak of their own spirit, supposing that it proceeded from the Spirit of prophecy." [31]What is this but to question the truth of all prophetical revelations, and to shake the faith that is built upon it? Surely the prophet Jeremiah had an infallible assurance of the author of his message, when he pleaded for himself before the princes,

> "Of a truth the LORD hath sent me unto you to speak all these words in your ears," chapter 26:15.

And Abraham certainly had need of a good assurance whence that motion did proceed which made him address himself to the sacrificing the son of promise. And that all other prophets had the like evidence of knowledge concerning the divine verity of their revelations is unquestionable. Hence are those allusions in the Scripture, whereby it is compared unto things whereof we may be most certain by the assurance of sense. So Amos 3:8,

> "The lion hath roared, who will not fear? the Lord GOD hath spoken, who can but prophesy?"

---

[31] "Sciendum est quod aliquando prophetæ sancti dum consuluntur, ex magno usu prophetandi quædam ex suo spiritu proferunt, et se hoc ex prophetiæ spiritu dicere suspicantur." — *Greg. Hom. i. in Ezek.*

and Jeremiah 20:9, "His word was in mine heart as a burning fire shut up in my bones;" — things sensible enough. Haply Satan may so far delude false prophets as to make them suppose their lying vanities are from above; whence they are said to be "prophets of the deceit of their own heart," Jeremiah 23:26, being deceived as well as deceivers, thinking in themselves as well as speaking unto others, "He saith," verse 31. But that any true prophets should not know a true revelation from a motion of their own hearts wants not much of blasphemy. The Lord surely supposes that assurance of discerning when he gives that command,

> "The prophet that hath a dream, let him tell a dream; and he that hath my word, let him speak my word faithfully. What is the chaff to the wheat?" Jeremiah 23:28.

He must be both blind and mad that shall mistake wheat for chaff, and on the contrary. What some men speak of a hidden instinct from God moving the minds of men, yet so as they know not whether. it be from him or no, may better serve to illustrate Plutarch's discourse of Socrates' demon than any passage in holy writ. St Austin says his mother would affirm, that though she could not express it, yet she could discern the difference between God's revelation and her own dreams;[32] in which relation I doubt not but the learned father took advantage, from the good old woman's

---

[32] "Dicebat se discernere (nescio quo sapore quem verbis explicare non poterat) quid interesset inter Deum revelantem et animam suam somniantem." — *Aug. Conf.*

47

words of what she could do, to declare what might be done of every one that had such immediate revelations. Briefly, then; the Spirit of God never so extraordinarily moveth the mind of man to apprehend any thing of this kind whereof we speak, but it also illustrateth it with a knowledge and assurance that it is divinely moved to this apprehension. Now, because it is agreed on all sides that light prophetical is no permanent habit in the minds of the prophets, but a transient impression, of itself not apt to give any such assurance, it may be questioned from what other principle it doth proceed. But, not to pry into things perhaps not fully revealed, and seeing St Paul shows us that, in such heavenly raptures, there are some things unutterable of them and incomprehensible of us, we may let this rest amongst those ἄῤῥητα. It appeareth, then, from the preceding discourse, that a man pretending to extraordinary vocation by immediate revelation, in respect of self-persuasion of the truth of his call, must be as ascertained of it as he could be of a burning fire in his bones, if there shut up.

CHAPTER 6

*What assurance men extraordinarily called
can give to others that they are so called in the
former way.*

THE next thing to be considered is, what assurance
he can give to others, and by what means, that he is so
called. Now, the matter or subject of their employment
may give us some light to this consideration; and this
is, either the inchoation of some divine work to be
established amongst men, by virtue of a new and never-
before-heard-of revelation of God's will, or a restoration
of the same, when collapsed and corrupted by the sin
of men. To the first of these: God never sendeth any
but whom he doth so extraordinarily and immediately
call and ordain for that purpose; and that this may be
manifested unto others, he always accompanieth them
with his own almighty power, in the working of such
miracles as may make them be believed, for the very
works' sake which God by them doth effect. This we
may see in Moses and (after Jesus Christ, anointed
with the oil of gladness above his fellows to preach the
gospel) the apostles.

But this may pass, for nothing in such a way shall
ever again take place, God having ultimately revealed his
mind concerning his worship and our salvation, a curse
being denounced to man or angel that shall pretend to
revelation for the altering or changing one jot or tittle

of the gospel. For the other, the work of reformation, there being, ever since the writing of his word, an infallible rule for the performance of it, making it fall within the duty and ability of men partaking of an ordinary vocation, and instructed with ordinary gifts, God doth not always immediately call men unto it; but yet, because oftentimes he hath so done, we may inquire what assurance they could give of this their calling to that employment. Our Savior Christ informs us that a prophet is often without honor in his own country. The honor of a prophet is to have credence given to his message (of which, it should seem, Jonah was above measure zealous); yet such is the cursed infidelity and hardness of men's hearts, that though they cried, "Thus saith the LORD," yet they would reply, "The LORD hath not spoken." Hence are those pleadings betwixt the prophet Jeremiah and his enemies; the prophet averring, "Of a truth the LORD hath sent me unto you," and they contesting that the LORD had not sent him, but that he lied in the name of the LORD. Now, to leave them inexcusable, and, whether they would hear or whether they would forbear, to convince them that there hath been a prophet amongst them, as also to give the greater credibility to their extraordinary message to them that were to believe their report, it is necessary that "the arm of the LORD should be revealed," working in and by them in some extraordinary manner. It is certain enough that God never sent any one extraordinarily, instructed only with ordinary gifts and for an ordinary end. The aim of their employment I showed before was extraordinary, even the reparation of something instituted by God and collapsed by the sin of man. That it may be credible, or appear of a truth that God had sent them for this purpose, they were always furnished with such gifts and abilities as the utmost reach of human endeavors, with the assistance of common grace, cannot possibly attain. The general opinion is, that God always supplies such with the gift of miracles. Take the word in a large sense, for every supernatural product, beyond the ordinary activity of that secondary cause whereby it is effected, and I easily grant it; but in the usual restrained acceptation of it, for outward wonderful works, the power of whose production consists in operation, I something doubt the universal truth of the assertion. We do not read of any such miracles wrought by the prophet Amos, and yet he stands upon his extraordinary immediate vocation, "I was no prophet, neither was I a prophet's son, but the LORD took me," etc. It sufficeth, then, that they be furnished with a supernatural power, either in,

1. Discerning;
2. Speaking; or
3. Working.

First, The power of discerning, according to the things by it discernible, may be said to be of two sorts: for it is either of things present, beyond the power of human investigation, as to know the thoughts of other men's hearts, or their words not ordinarily to be known, — as Elisha discovered the bed-chamber discourse of the king of Syria (not that by virtue of their calling they come to be καρδιογνώσται, "knowers of the heart," which is God's property alone, but that God doth sometimes reveal such things unto them; for otherwise no such power is included in the nature of the gift, which is perfective of their knowledge, not by the way of habit, but actual motion in respect of some particulars; and when this was absent, the same Elisha affirmeth that he knew not why the Shunammitish woman was troubled); or, secondly, of things future and contingent in respect of their secondary causes, not precisely necessitated by their own internal principle of operation for the effecting of the things so foreknown; and, therefore, the truth of the foreknowledge consists in a commensuration to God's purpose. Now, effects of this power are all those predictions of such things which we find in the Old and New Testament, and divers also since. Secondly, The supernatural gift in speaking I intimate is that of tongues, proper to the times of the gospel, when the worship of God was no longer to be confined to the people of one nation. The third, working, is that which strictly and properly is called the gift of miracles, which are hard, rare, and strange effects, exceeding the whole order of created nature, for whose production God sometimes useth his servants instrumentally, moving and enabling them thereunto by a transient impression of his powerful grace; of which sort the holy Scripture hath innumerable relations. Now, with one of those extraordinary gifts at least, sometimes with all, doth the Lord furnish those his messengers of whom we treat; which makes their message a sufficient revelation of God's will, and gives it credibility enough to stir up faith in some, and leave others inexcusable. All the difficulty is, that there have been Simon Maguses, and there are Antichrists, falsely pretending to have in themselves this mighty power of God, in one or other of the forenamed kinds. Hence were those many false prophets, dreamers, and wizards mentioned in the Old Testament, which the Lord himself forewarns us of; as also those agents of that man of sin, "whose coming is after the working of Satan, with all power and signs and lying wonders," 2 Thessalonians 2:9. I mean the juggling priests and Jesuits, pretending falsely by their impostures to the power of miracleworking, though their employment be not to reform, but professedly to corrupt the worship of God. Now, in such a case as this, we have, —

1. The *mercy of God* to rely upon, whereby he will guide his into the way of truth; and the purpose or decree of God, making it impossible that his elect should be deceived by them.

2. *Human diligence*, accompanied with God's blessing, may help us wonderfully in a discovery whether the pretended miracles be of God or no, for there is nothing more certain than that a true and real miracle is beyond the activity of all created power (for if it be not, it is not a miracle); so that the devil and all his emissaries are not able to effect any one act truly miraculous, but in all their pretences there is a defect discernible, either in respect of the thing itself pretended to be done, or of the manner of its doing, not truly exceeding the power of art or nature, though the apprehension of it, by reason of some hell-conceived circumstances, be above our capacity. Briefly: either

the thing is a lie, and so it is easy to feign miracles; or the performance of it is pure juggling, and so it is easy to delude poor mortals. Innumerable of this sort, at the beginning of the Reformation, were discovered among the agents of that wonder-working "man of sin," by the blessing of God upon human endeavours. Now, from such discoveries a good conclusion may be drawn against the doctrine they desire by such means to confirm; for as God never worketh true miracles but for the confirmation of the truth, so will not men pretend such as are false, but to persuade that to others for a truth which themselves have just reason to be persuaded is a lie. Now, if this means fail, —

3. God himself hath set down a rule of direction for us in the time of such difficulty: Deuteronomy 13:1-5,

> "If there arise among you a prophet, or a dreamer of dreams, and giveth thee a sign or a wonder, and the sign or the wonder come to pass, whereof he spake unto thee, saying, Let us go after other gods, which thou hast not known, and let us serve them; thou shalt not hearken unto the words of that prophet, or that dreamer of dreams: for the LORD your God proveth you, to know whether ye love the LORD your God with all your heart and with all your soul. Ye shall walk after the LORD your God, and fear him, and keep his commandments, and obey his voice, and ye shall serve him, and cleave unto him. And that prophet, or that dreamer of dreams, shall be put to death."

The sum is, that seeing such men pretend that their revelations and miracles are from heaven, let us search whether the doctrine they seek to confirm by them be from heaven or no. If it be not, let them be stoned or accursed, for they seek to draw us from our God; if it be, let not the curse of a stony heart, to refuse them, be upon us. Where the miracles are true, the doctrine cannot be false; and if the doctrine be true, in all probability the miracles confining it are not false. And so much of them who are immediately called of God from heaven, [as to] what assurance they may have in themselves of such a call, and what assurance they can make of it to others. Now, such are not to expect any ordinary vocation from men below, God calling them aside to his work from the midst of their brethren. The Lord of the harvest may send laborers into his field without asking his steward's consent, and they shall speak whatever he saith unto them.

CHAPTER 7

The second way whereby a man may be called extraordinarily.

SECONDLY, A mail may be extraordinarily called to the preaching and publishing of God's word by a concurrence of Scripture rules, directory for such occasions, occurrences, and opportunities of time, place, and persons, as he liveth in and under. Rules in this kind may be drawn either from express precept or approved practice. Some of these I shall intimate, and leave it to the indifferent reader to judge whether or no they hold in the application; and all that in this kind I shall propose, I do with submission to better judgments.

1. Consider, then, that of our Savior to St Peter, Luke 22:32, "When thou art converted, strengthen thy brethren;" which containing nothing but an application of one of the prime dictates of the law of nature, cannot, ought not, to be restrained unto men of any peculiar calling as such. Not to multiply many of this kind (whereof in the Scripture is plenty), add only that of St James, James 5:19,20,

> "Brethren, if any of you do err from the truth, and one convert him, let him know, that he which converteth the sinner from the error of his way shall save a soul from death," etc.

From these and the like places it appears to me, that, —

There is a general obligation on all Christians to promote the conversion and instruction of sinners, and men erring from the right way.

2. Again, consider that of our Savior, Matthew 5:15,

> "Men do not light a candle and put it under a bushel, but on a candlestick, and it giveth light unto all that are in the house;"

to which add that of the apostle,

> "If any thing be revealed to another that sitteth by, let the first hold his peace," 1 Corinthians 14:30:

which words, although primarily they intend extraordinary immediate revelations, yet I see no reason why in their equity and extent they may not be directory for the use of things revealed unto us by Scripture light. At least, we may deduce from them, by the way of analogy, that, —

Whatsoever necessary truth is revealed to any out of the word of God, not before known, he ought to have an uncontradicted liberty of declaring that truth, provided that he use such regulated ways for that his declaration as the church wherein he liveth (if a right church) cloth allow.

3. Farther, see Amos 3:8,

> "The lion hath roared, who will not fear? the Lord GOD hath spoken, who can but prophesy?"

and Jeremiah 20:9,

"Then I said, I will not make mention of him, nor speak any more in his name. But his word was in mine heart as a burning fire shut up in my bones; and I was weary with forbearing, and I could not stay;"

with the answer of Peter and John to the rulers of the Jews, Acts 4:19,20,

"Whether it be right in the sight of God to hearken unto you more than unto God, judge ye; for we cannot but speak the things which we have seen and heard."

Whence.it appears, that, —

Truth revealed unto any carries along with it an unmovable persuasion of conscience (which is powerfully obligatory) that it ought to be published and spoken to others.

That none may take advantage of this to introduce confusion into our congregations, I gave a sufficient caution in the second rule.

Many other observations giving light to the business in hand might be taken from the common dictates of nature, concurring with many general precepts we have in the Scripture, but, omitting them, the next thing I propose is the practice, etc., —

1. Of our Savior Christ himself, who did not only pose the doctors when he was but twelve years old, Luke 2:46, but also afterward preached in the synagogue of Nazareth, chapter 4:16-22, being neither doctor, nor scribe, nor Levite, but of the tribe of Judah (concerning which tribe it is evident that Moses spake nothing concerning the priesthood).

2. Again, in the eighth of the Acts, great persecution arising against the church after the death of Stephen, "they were all scattered abroad from Jerusalem," verse 1, — that is, all the faithful members of the church, — who being thus dispersed, "went everywhere preaching the word," verse 4; and to this their publishing of the gospel (having no warrant but the general engagement of all Christians to further the propagation of Christ's kingdom), occasioned by their own persecution, the Lord gave such a blessing, that they were thereby the first planters of a settled congregation among the Gentiles, they and their converts being the first that were honored by the name of Christians, Acts 11:21,26.

3. Neither is the example of St Paul altogether impertinent, who with his companions repaired unto the synagogues of the Jews, and taught them publicly, yea, upon their own request, Acts 13:15. Apollos also spake boldly and preached fervently when he knew only the baptism of John, and needed himself farther instruction. Acts 18:24-26. It should seem, then, in that juncture of time, he that was instructed in any truth not ordinarily known might publicly acquaint others with it, though he himself were ignorant in other points of high concernment; yet, perhaps, now it is not possible that any occurrences should require a precise imitation of what was not only lawful but also expedient in that dawning towards the clear day of the last unchangeable revelation of God's will. Now, in these and the like there is so much variety, such several grounds and circumstances, that no direct rule can from them be drawn; only, they may give strength to

what from the former shall be concluded.

For a farther light to this discourse, consider what desolate estate the church of God hath been, may be, and at this present in divers places is, reduced to. Her silver may become dross, and her wine be mixed with water, the faithful city becoming a harlot; her shepherds may be turned into dumb, sleeping dogs, and devouring wolves; the watchmen may be turned smiters, her prophets to prophesy falsely, and her priests to bear rule by lies; the commandments of God being made void by the traditions of men, superstition, human inventions, will-worship, may defile and contaminate the service of God; yea, and greater abominations may men possessing Moses' chair by succession do.[33] Now, that the temple of God hath been thus made a den of thieves, that the abomination of desolation hath been set up in the holy place, is evident from the Jewish and Christian church; for in the one it was clearly so when the government of it was devolved to the scribes and Pharisees, and in the other when the man of sin had exalted himself in the midst thereof. Now, suppose a man living in the midst and height of such a sad apostasy, when a universal darkness had spread itself over the face of the church; if the Lord be pleased to reveal unto him out of his word some points of faith, then either not at all known or generally disbelieved, yet a right belief whereof is necessary to salvation; and, farther, out of the same word shall discover unto him the wickedness of that apostasy, and the means to remove

---

[33] Ezek. xxii. 27, 28, viii. 13.

it, — I demand whether that man, without expecting any call from the fomenters and maintainers of those errors with which the church at that time is only not destroyed, may not preach, publish, and publicly declare the said truths to others (the knowledge of them being so necessary for the good of their souls), and conclude himself thereunto called of God, by virtue of the fore-named and other the like rules? Truly, for my part (under correction), I conceive he may, nay, he ought; neither is any other outward call requisite to constitute him a preacher of the gospel than the consent of God's people to be instructed by him. For instance: suppose that God should reveal the truth of the gospel to "a mere layman" (as they say) in Italy, so that he be fully convinced thereof, what shall he now do? abstain from publishing it, though he be persuaded in conscience that a great door of utterance might be granted unto him, only because some heretical, simoniacal, wicked, antichristian prelate hath not ordained him minister, who yet would not do it unless he will subscribe to those errors and heresies which he is persuaded to be such? Truly, I think by so abstaining he should sin against *the law of charity*, in seeing, not the ox or ass of his brother falling into the pit, but their precious souls sinking to everlasting damnation, and not preventing it when he might; and were he indeed truly angry with his whole nation, he might have the advantage of an Italian revenge.

Moreover, he should sin against the precept of Christ, by hiding his light under a bushel, and napkening up his talent, an increase whereof will be required of him at the last day. Now, with this I was always so well satisfied, that I ever deemed all curious disquisition after the outward vocation of our first reformers, Luther, Calvin, etc, altogether needless, the case in their days being exactly that which I have laid down.

Come we now to the THIRD and last way whereby men, not partakers of any outward ordinary vocation, may yet receive a sufficient warrant for the preaching and publishing of the gospel, and that by some outward act of Providence guiding them thereunto. For example: put case a Christian man should, by any chance of providence, be cast, by shipwreck, or otherwise upon the country of some barbarous people that never heard of the name of Christ, and there, by His goodness that brought him thither, be received amongst them into civil human society, may he not, nay, ought he not, to preach Christ unto them? and if God give a blessing to his endeavors, may he not become a pastor to the converted souls? None, I hope, makes any doubt of it; and in the primitive times nothing was more frequent than such examples. Thus were the Indians and the Moors turned to the faith, as you may see in Eusebius; yea, great was the liberty which in the first church was used in this kind, presently after the supernatural gift of tongues ceased amongst men.

CHAPTER 8

Of the liberty and duty of gifted uncalled Christians in the exercise of divers acts of God's worship.

AND thus have I declared what I conceive concerning extraordinary calling to the public teaching of the word, in what cases only it useth to take place; whence I conclude, that whosoever pretends unto it, not warranted by an evidence of one of those three ways that God taketh in such proceedings, is but a pretender, an impostor, and ought, accordingly, to be rejected of all God's people. In other cases, not to disuse what outward ordinary occasion, from them who are intrusted by commission from God with that power, doth confer upon persons so called, we must needs grant it a negative voice in the admission of any to the public preaching of the gospel. If they come not in at that door, they do climb over the wall, if they make any entrance at all. It remains, then, to shut up all, that it be declared what private Christians, living in a pure, orthodox, well-ordered church, may do, and how far they may interest themselves in holy, soul- concerning affairs, both in respect of their own particular and of their brethren in the midst of whom they live; in which determination, because it concerneth men of low degree, and those that comparatively may be said to be unlearned, I shall labor to express the conceivings of my mind in as familiar, plain observations as I can. Only, thus much I desire may be premised, that the principles and rules of that church government from which, in the following assertions, I desire not to wander are of that kind (to which I do, and always, in my poor judgment, have adhered, since, by God's assistance, I had engaged myself to the study of his word) which commonly are called presbyterial or synodical, in opposition to prelatical or diocesan on the one side, and that which is commonly called independent or congregational on the other.

First, then, a *diligent searching* of the Scriptures, with fervent prayers to Almighty God for the taking away that veil of ignorance which by nature is before their eyes, that they may come to a saving knowledge in and a right understanding of them, is not only *lawful* and *convenient* for all men professing the name of Christ, but also absolutely *necessary;* because *commanded*, yea indeed commanded, because the end so to be attained is absolutely necessary to salvation. To confirm this I need not multiply precepts out of the Old or New Testament, (such as that of Isaiah 8:20, "To the law and to the testimony;" and that of John 5:39, "Search the Scriptures,") which are innumerable; nor yet heap up motives unto it, such as are the description of the heavenly country whither we are going, in them contained, John 14:2; 2 Corinthians 5:1; Revelation 22:1, etc.; the way by which we are to travel, laid down John 5:39, 14:5, 6; Jesus Christ, whom we must labor to be like, painted out, Galatians 3:1; and the back parts of God discovered, Deuteronomy 29:29. By them only true spiritual wisdom is conveyed to our souls, Jeremiah 8:9, whereby we may become even wiser than our teachers, Psalm 119:99; in them all comfort and consolation is to be had in the time of danger and trouble, Psalm 119:54,71,72; in brief, the knowledge of Christ, which is "life eternal," John 17:3; yea, all that can be said in this kind comes infinitely short of those treasures of wisdom, riches, and goodness which are contained in them:

> "The law of the LORD is perfect, converting the soul; the testimony of the LORD is sure, making wise the simple," Psalm 19:7.

But this duty of the people is clear and confessed, the objections of the Papists against it being, for the most part, so many blasphemies against the holy word of God. They accuse it of difficulty, which God affirms to "make wise the simple;" of obscurity, which "openeth the eyes of the blind;" to be a dead letter, a nose of wax, which is "quick and powerful, piercing to the dividing asunder of the soul and spirit;" to be weak and insufficient, which "is able to make the man of God perfect" and "wise unto salvation." Yea, that word which the apostle affirmeth to be "profitable for reproof" is not in any thing more full than in reproving of this blasphemy.

Secondly, They may not only (as before) search the Scriptures, but also examine and *try by them the doctrine that publicly is taught unto them.* The people of God must not be like

> "children, tossed to and fro, and carried about

with every wind of doctrine, by the sleight of men, and cunning craftiness, whereby they lie in wait to deceive," Ephesians 4:14.

All is not presently gospel that is spoken in the pulpit; it is not long since that altar-worship, Arminianism, Popery, superstition, etc., were freely preached in this kingdom. Now, what shall the people of God do in such a case? Yield to every breath, to every puff of false doctrine? or rather try it by the word of God, and if it be not agreeable thereunto, cast it out like salt that hath lost its savor? Must not the people take care that they be not seduced? Must they not "beware of false prophets, which come unto them in sheep's clothing, but inwardly are ravening wolves?" And how shall they do this? what way remains but a trying their doctrine by the rule? In these evil days wherein we live, I hear many daily complaining that there is such difference and contrariety among preachers, they know not what to do nor scarce what to believe. My answer is, Do but your own duty, and this trouble is at an end. Is there any contrariety in the book of God? Pin not your faith upon men's opinions; the Bible is the touchstone. That there is such diversity amongst teachers is their fault, who should think all the same thing; but that this is so troublesome to you is your own fault, for neglecting your duty of trying all things by the word. Alas! you are in a miserable condition, if you have all this while relied on the authority of men in heavenly things. He that builds his faith upon preachers, though they preach nothing but truth, and he pretend to believe it, hath indeed no faith at all, but a wavering opinion, built upon a rotten foundation. Whatever, then, is taught you, you must go with it

> "to the law and to the testimony: if they speak not according to this word, it is because there is no light in them," Isaiah 8:20.

Yea, the Bereans are highly extolled for searching whether the doctrine concerning our Savior preached by St Paul were so or no, Acts 17:11; agreeably to the precept of the same preacher, 1 Thessalonians 5:21, "Prove all things, hold fast that which is good;" as also to that of John 4:1, "Beloved, believe not every spirit, but try the spirits whether they be of God; because many false prophets are gone out into the world." Prophets, then, must be tried before they be trusted. Now, the reason of this holds still. There are many false teachers abroad in the world; wherefore try every one, try his spirit, his spiritual gift of teaching, and that by the word of God. And here you have a clear rule laid down how you may extricate yourselves from the former perplexity. Nay, St Paul himself, speaking to understanding Christians, requires them to judge of it: 1 Corinthians 10:15, "I speak as to wise men; judge ye what I say." Hence are those cautions that the people should look that none do seduce them, Matthew 24:4; to which end they must have their souls "exercised" in the word of God, "to discern both good and evil," Hebrews 5:14. Thus, also, in one place Christ biddeth his followers hear the Pharisees, and do what they should command, because they sat in Moses' chair, Matthew 23:2,3; and yet in another place gives them a caution to beware of the doctrine of the Pharisees, Matthew 16:12. It remaineth, then, that the people are bound to hear those who possess the place of teaching in the church, but withal they must beware that it contain nothing of the old leaven; to which end they must try it by the word of God; when, as St Paul prayeth for the Philippians,

> "their love may abound yet more and more in knowledge, and all judgment, that they may approve things that are excellent," Philippians 1:9,10.

Unless ministers will answer for all those souls they shall mislead, and excuse them before God at the day of trial, they ought not to debar them from trying their doctrine. Now this they cannot do; for "if the blind lead the blind, both fall into the pit" of destruction. And here I might have just occasion of complaint: —

1. Of the superstitious pride of the late clergy of this land, who could not endure to have their doctrine tried by their auditors, crying to poor men, with the Pharisees, John 9:34,

> "'Ye were altogether born in sins, and do ye teach us?' A pretty world it is like to be, when the sheep will needs teach their pastors!"

Nothing would serve them but a blind submission to the loose dictates of their cobweb homilies. He saw farther, sure, in the darkness of Popery, who contended that a whole general council ought to give place to a simple layman urging Scripture or speaking reason. Now, surely this is very far from that gentleness, meekness, and aptness to teach, which St Paul requireth in a man of God, a minister of the gospel.

2. The negligence of the people, also, might here come under a just reproof, who have not labored to discern the voice of the hireling from that of the true shepherd, but have promiscuously followed the new-fangledness and heretical errors of every time-serving starver of souls. Whence proceedeth all that misery the land now groaneth under, but that we have had a people willing to be led by a corrupted clergy, freely drinking in the poison wherewith they are tainted? "The prophets prophesied falsely, the priests bare rule by their means, the people loved to have it so; but what shall we now do in the end thereof?" Who could ever have thought that the people of England would have yielded a willing ear to so many popish errors, and an obedient shoulder to such a heavy burden of superstitions, as in a few years were instilled into them, and laid upon them voluntarily, by their own sinful neglect, ensnaring their consciences by the omission of this duty we insist upon, of examining by the word what is taught unto them?[34] But this is no place for complaints. And this is a second thing which the people, distinct from their pastors, may do for their own edification. Now, whether they do this privately, every one apart, or by assembling more together, is altogether indifferent. And that this was observed by private Christians in the primitive times is very apparent.

Come we, in the third place, to what either their

---

[34] "Vos facite quod scriptum est, ut uno dicente, omnes examinent, me ergo dicente quod sentio, vos discernite et examinate." — *Orig, in Josh. Hom. xxi.*

duty binds them to, or otherwise by the word they are allowed to do, in sacred performances having reference to others. Look, then, in general upon those things we find them tied unto by virtue of special precept, such as are, to warn the unruly, comfort the feeble-minded, support the weak, 1 Thessalonians 5:14; to admonish and reprove offending brethren, Matthew 18:15; to instruct the ignorant, John 4:29, Acts 18:26; to exhort the negligent, Hebrews 3:13, 10:24,25; to comfort the afflicted, 1 Thessalonians 5:11; to restore him that falleth, Galatians 6:1; to visit the sick, Matthew 25:36,40; to reconcile those that are at variance, Matthew 5:9; to contend for the faith, Jude 3, 1 Peter 3:15; to pray for the sinner not unto death, 1 John 5:16; to edify one another in their most holy faith, Jude 20; to speak to themselves in psalms, and hymns, and spiritual songs, Ephesians 5:19; to be ready to answer every man in giving account of their faith, Colossians 4:6; to mark them that make divisions, Romans 16:17; with innumerable others to the like purpose.

It remaineth for them to consider, secondly, in particular, what course they may take, beyond private conference between man and man, by indiction of time or place for the fulfilling of what, by these precepts and the like, is of them required. To which I answer, —

First, lawful things must be done lawfully. If any unlawful circumstance attend the performance of a lawful action, it vitiates the whole work; for "bonum oritur ex integris." For instance, to reprove an offender is a Christian duty, but for a private man to do it in the public congregation whilst the minister is preaching, were, instead of a good act, a foul crime, being a notorious disturbance of church decency and order.

Secondly, That for a public, formal, ministerial teaching, two things are required in the teacher: — first, Gifts from God; secondly, Authority from the church (I speak now of ordinary cases). He that wants either is no true pastor. For the first, God sends none upon an employment but whom he fits with gifts for it,

1. Not one command in the Scripture made to teachers;
2. Not one rule for their direction;
3. Not one promise to their endeavors;
4. Not any end of their employment;
5. Not one encouragement to their duty;
6. Not one reproof for their negligence;
7. Not the least intimation of their reward, — but cuts off ungifted, idle pastors from any true interest in the calling.

And for the others, that want authority from the church, neither ought they to undertake any formal act properly belonging to the ministry, such as is solemn teaching of the word; for, —

1. They are none of Christ's officers, Ephesians 4:11.
2. They are expressly forbidden it, Jeremiah 23:21; Hebrews 5:4.
3. The blessing on the word is promised only to sent teachers, Romans 10:14,15.
4. If to be gifted be to be called, then, —

(1.) Every one might undertake so much in sacred duties as he fancies himself to be able to perform;

(2.) Children (as they report of Athanasius[35]) might baptize;

(3.) Every common Christian might administer the communion. But endless are the arguments that might be multiplied against this fancy. In a word, if our Savior Christ be the God of order, he hath left his church to no such confusion.

Thirdly, That to appoint time and place for the doing of that which God hath appointed indefinitely to be done in time and place, rather commends than vitiates the duty. So did Job's friends in the duty of comforting the afflicted; they made an appointment together to come and comfort him, Job 2:11; and so did they, Zechariah 8:21; and so did David, Psalm 119:62.

Fourthly, There is much difference between opening or interpreting the word, and applying the word upon the advantage of such an approved interpretation; as also between an authoritative act, or doing a thing by virtue of special office, and a charitable act, or doing a thing out of a motion of Christian love. ,

Fifthly, It may be observed concerning gifts, —

1. That the gifts and graces of God's Spirit are of two sorts, some being bestowed for the sanctification of God's people, some for the edification of his church; some of a private allay, looking primarily inwards to the

---

[35] Eusebius, Ruf.

saving of his soul on whom they are bestowed (though in their fruits also they have a relation and habitude to others), other some aiming at the commonwealth or profit of the whole church as such. Of the first sort are those mentioned Galatians 5:22,23, "The fruit of the Spirit is love, joy, peace," etc., with all other graces that are necessary to make the man of God perfect in all holiness and the fear of the Lord; the other are those χαρισματα πνευματικα, spiritual gifts of teaching, praying, prophesying, mentioned 1 Corinthians 14, and in other places.

2. That all these gifts, coming down from the Father of lights, are given by the same Spirit, "dividing to every man severally as he will," 1 Corinthians 12:11. He is not tied, in the bestowing of his gifts, to any sort, estate, calling, or condition of men; but worketh them freely, as it pleaseth him, in whom he will. The Spirit them mentioned is that God which "worketh all things after the counsel of his own will," Ephesians 1:11; they are neither deserved by our goodness nor obtained by our endeavors.

3. That the end why God bestoweth these gifts on any is merely that, within the bounds of their own calling (in which they are circumscribed, 1 Corinthians 1:26), they should use them to his glory and the edification of his church; for "the manifestation of the Spirit is given to every man to profit withal," 1 Corinthians 12:7. Christ gives none of his talents to be bound up in napkins, but expects his own with increase.[36]

---

[36] Eccles. xii. 9.

And from these considerations it is easily discernible both what the people of God, distinct from their pastors, in a well-ordered church, may do in this kind whereof we treat, and how. In general, then, I assert, —

That, for the improving of knowledge, the increasing of Christian charity, for the furtherance of a strict and holy communion of that spiritual love and amity which ought to be amongst the brethren, they may of their own accord assemble together, to consider one another, to provoke unto love and good works, to stir up the gifts that are in them, yielding and receiving mutual consolation by the fruits of their most holy faith.

Now, because there be many Uzzahs amongst us, who have an itching desire to be fingering of the ark, thinking more highly of themselves than they ought to think, and, like the ambitious sons of Levi, taking too much upon them, it will not be amiss to give two cautions, deducted from the former rules: —

First, That they do not, under a pretense of Christian liberty and freedom of conscience, cast away all brotherly amity, and cut themselves off from the communion of the church. Christ hath not purchased a liberty for any to rend his body. They will prove at length to be no duties of piety which break the sacred bonds of charity.

Men ought not, under a pretense of congregating themselves to serve their God, separate from their brethren, neglecting the public assemblies; as was the manner of some rebuked by the apostle, "'Hebrews 10:25. There be peculiar blessings and transcendent privileges annexed to public assemblies, which accompany not private men to their recesses. The sharp-edged sword becomes more keen when set on by a skillful master of the assemblies; and when the water of the word flows there, the Spirit of God moves upon the face thereof, to make it effectual in our hearts.

"What! despise ye the church of God?" 1 Corinthians 11:22.

Secondly, As the ministry, so also ought the ministers to have that regard, respect, and obedience, which is due to their labors in that sacred calling. Would we could not too frequently see more puffed up with the conceit of their own gifts, into a contempt of the most learned and pious pastors! — these are "spots in your feasts of charity, clouds without water, carried about of winds." It must, doubtless, be an evil root that bringeth forth such bitter fruit. Wherefore, let not our brethren fall into this condemnation, lest there be an evil report raised by them that are without; but

> "remember them which have the rule over you, who have spoken unto you the word of God," Hebrews 13:7.

There is no greater evidence of the heavenly improvement you make by your recesses than that you obey them that are guides unto you, and submit yourselves: for "they watch for your souls, as they that must give an account, that they may do it with joy, and not with grief: for that is unprofitable for you," verse 17. Let not them who despise a faithful, painful minister in public, flatter themselves with hope of a blessing on their endeavors in private. Let them pretend what they will, they have not an equal respect unto all God's ordinances. Wherefore, that the coming together in this sort may be for the better, and not for the worse, observe these things: —

Now, for what gifts (that are, as before, freely bestowed) whose exercise is permitted unto such men so assembled; I mean in a private family, or two or three met ὁμοθυμαδόν, in one.

And first we may name the gift of prayer, whose exercise must not be exempted from such assemblies, if any be granted. These are the times wherein the Spirit of grace and of supplications is promised to be poured out upon the Jerusalem of God, Zechariah 12:10. Now, God having bestowed the gift and requiring the duty, his people ought not to be hindered in the performance of it. Are all those precepts to pray, in the

Scriptures, only for our closets? When the church was in distress for the imprisonment of Peter, there was a meeting at the house of Mary, the mother of John, Acts 12:12. "Many were gathered together praying," saith the text; — a sufficient warrant for the people of God in like cases. The churches are in no less distress now than at that time; and in some congregations the ministers are so oppressed that publicly they dare not, in others so corrupted that they will not, pray for the prosperity of Jerusalem Now, truly, it were a disconsolate thing for any one of God's servants to say, "During all these straits, I never joined with any of God's children in the pouring out of my prayer in the behalf of his church:" neither can I see how this can possibly be prevented but by the former means; to which add the counsel of St Paul,

> "Speaking to themselves in psalms and hymns and spiritual songs, singing and making melody in their hearts unto the Lord," Ephesians 5:19.

Secondly, They may exercise the gifts of *wisdom, knowledge,* and *understanding* in the ways of the Lord; comforting, strengthening, and encouraging each other with the same consolations and promises which, by the benefit of the public ministry, they have received from the word. Thus, in time of distress, the prophet Malachi tells us that

> "they that feared the LORD spake often one to another, and the LORD hearkened, and heard," etc., chapter 3:16;

— comforting, as it appears, one another in the promises of God made unto his church, against the flourishing of the wicked and overflowing of ungodliness, the persecution of tyrants and impurity of transgressors.

Thirdly, They may make *use of "the tongue of the learned"* (if given unto them) to "speak a word in season to him that is weary," Isaiah 50:4; for being commanded to "confess their faults one to another," James 5:16, they have power also to apply to them that are penitent the promises of mercy. We should never be commanded to open our wounds to them who have no balm to pour into them; he shall have cold comfort who seeks for counsel from a dumb man. So that in this, and the like cases, they may apply unto and instruct one another in the word of God; doing it as a charitable duty, and not as out of necessary function, even as Aquila and Priscilla expounded unto Apollos the word of God more perfectly than he knew it before, Acts 18:24-26. In sum, and not to enlarge this discourse with any more particulars, the people of God are allowed all quiet and peaceable means, whereby they may help each other forward in the knowledge of godliness and the way towards heaven.

Now, for the close of this discourse, I will remove some objections that I have heard godly men, and men not unlearned, lay against it, out of a zeal (not unlike that of Joshua for Moses' sake) [for] the constitute pastor's sake; to whom, though I might briefly answer, with Moses, "'Would God all the LORD's people were prophets!' — I heartily wish that every one of them had such a plentiful measure of spiritual endowments that they might become wise unto salvation, above many of their teachers;" in which vote I make no doubt but every one will concur with me who has the least experimental knowledge what a burden upon the shoulders, what a grief unto the soul of a minister knowing and desiring to discharge his duty, is an ignorant congregation (of which, thanks to our prelates, pluralists, nonresidents, homilies, service-book, and ceremonies, we have too many in this kingdom; the many, also, of our ministers in this church taking for their directory the laws and penalties of men, informing what they should not do if they would avoid their punishment, and not the precepts of God, what they should as their duty do if they meant to please him, and knowing there was no statute whereon they might be sued for (pardon the expression) the dilapidation of souls: so their own houses were ceiled, they cared not at all though the church of God lay waste); — I say, though I might thus answer, with opening my desire for the increasing of knowledge among the people, of which I take this to be an effectual means, yet I will give brief answers to the several objections: —

> **Objection 1.** "Then this seems to favor all allowance of licentious conventicles, which in all places the laws have condemned, and learned men in all ages have abhorred, as the seminaries of faction and schism in the church of God."

Ans. That (under correction) I conceive the law layeth hold of none, as peccant in such a kind, but only those who have pre-declared themselves to be opposers of the worship of God in the public assemblies of that church wherein they live. Now, the patronage of any such I before rejected. Neither do I conceive that they ought at all to be allowed the benefit of private meetings who wilfully abstain from the public congregations, so long as the true worship of God is held forth in them. Yea, how averse I have ever been from that kind of confused licentiousness in any church, I have some while since declared, in an answer (drawn up for my own and private friends' satisfaction) to the arguments of the Remonstrants in their Apology, and replies to Vedelius, with other treatises, for such a "liberty of prophesying," as they term it, If, then, the law account only such assemblies to be conventicles wherein the assemblers contemn and despise the service of God in public, I have not spoken one word in favor of them.

And for that canon which was mounted against them, whether intentionally, in the first institution of it, it was moulded and framed against Anabaptists or no, I cannot tell; but this I am sure, that in the discharge of it, it did execution oftentimes upon such as had Christ's precept and promise to warrant their assembling, Matthew 18:19,20. Not to contend about words, would to God that which is good might not be persecuted under odious appellations, and called evil when it is otherwise; so to expose it to the tyrannical oppression of the enemies of the gospel! The thing itself, rightly understood, can scarce be condemned of any who envies not the salvation of souls. They that would banish the gospel from our houses would not much care if it were gone from our hearts; from our houses, I say, for it is all one whether these duties be performed in one family or a collection of more. Some one is bigger than ten others; shall their assembling to perform what is lawful for that one be condemned for a conventicle? Where is the law for that? or what is there in all this more than God required of his ancient people, as I showed before? Or must a master of a family cease praying in his family, and instructing his children and servants in the ways of the Lord, for fear of being counted a preacher in a tub? Things were scarcely carried with an equal hand for the kingdom of Christ, when orders came forth on the one side to give liberty to the profane multitude to assemble themselves at heathenish sports, with bestial exclamations, on the Lord's own day; and on the other, to punish them who durst gather themselves together for prayer or the singing of psalms But I hope, through

God's blessing, we shall be for ever quit of all such ecclesiastical discipline as must be exercised according to the interest of idle drones, whom it concerneth to see that there be none to try or examine their doctrine, or of superstitious innovators, who desire to obtrude their fancies upon the unwary people. Whence comes it that we have such an innumerable multitude of ignorant, stupid souls, unacquainted with the very principles of religion, but from the discountenancing of these means of increasing knowledge by men who would not labor to do it themselves? O that we could see the many swearers, and drunkards, and Sabbath-breakers, etc., in this nation, guilty only of this crime! Would the kingdom were so happy, the church so holy!

> **Obj. 2.** "Men are apt to pride themselves in their gifts, and flatter themselves in their performances, so that let them approach as nigh as the tabernacle, and you shall quickly have them encroaching upon the priest's office also, and, by an overweening of their own endeavors, create themselves pastors in separate congregations.

Ans. It cannot be but offenses will come, so long as there is malice in Satan and corruption in men. There is no doubt but there is danger of some such thing; but hereof the liberty mentioned is not the cause, but an accidental occasion only, no way blamable. Gifts must not be condemned because they may be abused. God-fearing men will remember Korah, knowing, as one says well, that "Uzzah had better ventured the falling than the fingering of the ark." They that truly love their souls will not suffer themselves to be carried

THE DUTY OF PASTORS

away by false conceit, so far as to help to overthrow the very constitution of any church by confusion, or the flourishing of it by ignorance; both which would certainly follow such courses. Knowledge if alone puffeth up, but joined to charity it edifieth.

> **Obj. 3.** "But may not this be a means for men to vent and broach their own private fancies unto others? to foment and cherish errors in one another? to give false interpretations of the word, there being no way to prevent it?"

Ans. For interpreting of the word I speak not, but applying of it, being rightly interpreted. And for the rest, would to God the complaints were not true of those things that have for divers years in this church been done publicly and outwardly according to order! But, that no inconvenience arise from hence, the care rests on them to whom the dispensation of the word is committed, whose sedulous endeavor to reprove and convince all unsound doctrine, not agreeing to the form of wholesome words, is the sovereign and only remedy to cure, or means to prevent, this evil. For the close of all, we may observe that those who are most offended and afraid lest others should encroach upon their callings are, for the most part, such as have almost deserted it themselves, neglecting their own employment, when they are the busiest of mortals in things of this world. To conclude, then, for what I have delivered in this particular, I conceive that I have the judgment and practice of the whole church of Scotland, agreeable to the word of God, for my warrant. Witness the act of their assembly at Edinburgh, anno

1641, wherewith the learned Rutherford concludes his defense of their discipline, with whose words I will shut up this discourse: "Our assembly, also, commandeth godly conference at all occasional meetings, or as God's providence shall dispose, as the word of God commandeth, providing none invade the pastor's office, to preach the word, who are not called thereunto by God and his church."

Τῷ Θεῷ ἀριστομεγίστῳ δόξα.